# Turning Ideas Into Profits

*"A beginners guide to starting a business."*

Ashton Eugene Thomas

# Dedication

This book is dedicated to everyone out there who is tired of the daily grind and has ambitions to make the life-changing decision of starting their own business. Never give up, or let go of those dreams!

# Acknowledgment

This book is dedicated to Timothy R. Thomas. The past fourteen years have seen some great times and some challenging times, but through it all, you were my rock and compass. I forever am in your debt.

To my mother, Kathy Garcia: Thank you for all you have done, and continue to do for me. I have learned many valuable life lessons from you, but above all, you have taught me humility. This has kept me grounded my entire life, yet taught me to always dream big.

To Ian Van Staeyen: Thank you for everything. I cherish our friendship and your input.

To Driftwood Coffee Co: Thank you for the quiet space where I have been able to spend countless hours writing, rewriting, and enjoying great coffee.

To Richard Garcia: Thanks for all the years of friendship we have had. You have been the one person in life who I know I can reach out to for anything.

# About the Author

Ashton Eugene Thomas grew up in the small town of Alamosa, Colorado. Growing up in a single-parent home with two brothers, Ashton quickly learned from his mother the value of hard work and dedication. At the age of sixteen, Ashton opened up his first business selling baseball and football cards in a small storefront in his hometown of Alamosa. Since then Ashton has been a Managing Partner and Founding Member of several businesses in Arizona.

# Preface

Turning Ideas into Profits – A self-help guide to starting a business was designed and written for everyone who has the passion for starting a business but who has zero knowledge on how to do so.

# Contents

Page Left Blank Intentionally

# Chapter 1
# Introduction

*"Your work is going to fill a large part of your life, and the only way to be truly satisfied is to do what you believe is great work. And the only way to do great work is to love what you do."*

**-Steve Jobs**

You have probably heard of Paul Mitchell hair products. However, did you know that this brand was co-founded by John Paul DeJoria? DeJoria was a person who spent most of his time on the streets. He was determined to fulfill his entrepreneurial vision having only $700 in hand and today, he is known as one of the greatest entrepreneurs of our time. He is a renowned philanthropist as well, supporting a number of different social causes.

The purpose of sharing DeJoria's story is to bring into your attention that entrepreneurship attracts people who have unique minds and strong personalities. I, myself, used to work for a law enforcement agency until 2010. While working for law enforcement, I realized that I wanted more and that I was not satisfied to work for someone else. This was not what I wanted to be doing for the rest of my life. That is when I took the brave decision of quitting my job and devoting my time and efforts into converting my idea into a business.

Most people fear the thought of quitting their jobs, but they are unaware that you cannot cut corners. Either you want to start a business, or you don't. To make your business work, you have to give your everything. That is what I did. Hence today, I am a proud owner of several successful businesses.

There is something very special about starting a new business. It is like becoming a parent. The sense of creating something new will amaze you. However, like a baby, your business will need your constant and undivided attention. It is going to be completely dependent on you for its welfare and growth. Your new venture will need a good supply of cash to fulfill its needs and requirements. This cash can be obtained through investments from customers. That being said, this book will help you in establishing your business and taking the required actions.

As your business grows, its demands will change. It will slowly and gradually develop and mature. Eventually, if you have nurtured it well, your business will be established enough to support you without you being involved in the operations daily. All businesses grow at different rates. It may take years for a part-time enterprise to develop, whereas it may take a shorter amount of time for a specific business to establish. Regardless of your entrepreneurial aspirations, this book will help you throughout your business' journey. It will help you nurture the seed of your business idea. You can use the tips to grow your business and learn from the experiences of those who have already completed the journey.

This book follows a sequence and the chapters are arranged in a manner that an individual with no knowledge of establishing a business prior to reading this book will end up following the best route. Each chapter illustrates the points and shows you how you can deal with specific issues or opportunities. Moreover, those who intend to start a business and aspire to make millions, then this book will help them in doing things differently in order to set-up a business that they can grow and maybe, even sell in the future. At the end of this book, you will have sufficient knowledge and information about starting a business. You can follow the text and run your own business or even guide other aspiring entrepreneurs. To begin with, let us look at the reasons why starting a business is beneficial.

## Why You Should Start Your Own Business

Are you getting thoughts of quitting your job and starting your own business but are not sure whether it is the right decision or not? Are you afraid that you might fail or go broke or have to live uncomfortably? Are you scared that you might be letting your loved ones down? Or you might not be able to live up to your own expectations?

When you start your work life, there are only a few people who have a *"plan"* about their lives. They get a job, work hard, do well and then a few years later, they wake up one day realizing that they were not meant to work 9 to 5. Not everyone plans on being an entrepreneur; however, for some people, they have this itch to start their own business. The reward of starting your own business is not just the amount of money that you will be earning; in fact, it is due to a number of other reasons. Change is never easy; however, it is liberating. Changing your work or your business is a powerful step to take in life. And working for yourself represents a whole new you. Once you have decided to set up your own business, you will need an entrepreneurial spirit. Following are the reasons as to why starting your own business might just be the best decision you will ever make in your life:

## You Will Delete the "What-Ifs" from Your Life

We all have a passion for something or the other. If we have the required talent to be good at what we are passionate about, then surely we will find ways to turn it into a career. However, the competition in the market is pretty tough, and the finances may not seem too feasible. Therefore, we stick to our 9-5 job because it becomes a secure source of income.

However, what if you are bored with your job? Or you are bored of working 9-5? What if you are no longer excited about going to work? What if you are looking forward to doing something that you are passionate about and having the freedom of working on your own conditions? Starting your own business is a scary step; however, it is a way of life that will get rid of the 'what-ifs' in your life. Moreover, it will help in getting rid of the uncertainties that you have formed in your head, especially if you are in your 20s and you don't have a family to feed. You have nothing to lose, but you do have a lot to gain.

## Your Learning Curve Will Accelerate Like Never Before

When starting your business, you will be learning a lot with each step you take. When you are an employee, you are learning more about your role and your industry. However, when you are your own boss, you have to learn everything related to your business. This includes knowledge about marketing, accounting, operations, and finance.

You will have to be up-to-date with the new technology, tools, consumer trends, and news related to the industry. Your learning skills will never be like they used to be. Before you even know it, you will become a lifelong learner who loves to take up challenges to learn about something new each day. You will take life as a progressive journey, just like you take your business.

**Your Thoughts will Become Independent, and You Will Learn to Trust your Instinct**

When you start your own business, you will be required to make certain decisions on the spot. Whether you are a sole proprietor or working with a business partner, you will have to make decisions without consulting your boss or team members. With time, you will eventually learn to make decisions on your own and become more decisive as you grow. You will learn to trust your instincts because no one knows your business as you do.

Waking up and knowing that every decision you make is entirely dependent on you is a feeling that is indescribable. You will not have to compromise with the opinions of others because you will be making your own decision and you will be responsible for it.

**You Will Be Motivated Every Day To Go To Work**

This is one of the main reasons as to why people are starting their own businesses. Nothing is more exciting than following one's passion and dreams. Yes, you may have some sleepless nights due to new thoughts, ideas, strategies, stalking your competitors, and dreaming about the future.

Even during the days when you are not making any sales, you will still be motivated to work, fix the problems, and ensure your sales are constant. That is because the business is yours, and you are the only person responsible for getting it up and running. You are not working for somebody else. Therefore, you will have to work hard and make things happen on your own. Once you carry out the required tasks in establishing your business, the reward is going to be totally worth it.

## You Understand What It Feels Like to Follow One's Passion

Some people will never understand why people decide to struggle instead of living a constant life. After you have started your own business, you will understand how it feels to follow your heart and pursue your dreams. The reward does not have to be money; it can be in being your own boss and creating something that you truly love.

During your journey, you will learn how important it is to sacrifice some external things that make you happy for things that will give you internal happiness, such as the success of your business.

## You Will Become More Daring and Fearless

You may find it a daunting task when starting your business. In order to be successful in your business, you will have to believe in yourself and make daring decisions from time to time. At each stage of your business, you have to be brave enough to make decisions on your own since no one else will make your decisions for you. When you become an entrepreneur, you will get rid of your limited beliefs and will broaden your horizon. You will gradually learn that your comfort zone keeps expanding every time you move away from it.

You will learn to make contacts and approach new people who are related to your industry. You will learn to make things happen even though you have no idea how to do them. You will also learn to do things the hard way, but then you will do them without a doubt and without any fear. With time, it would become a habit, and you will develop this boldness inside you. Ultimately, you will be able to get out of your comfort zone.

**You Will Become a Man of Actions and Not Just Words**

As an entrepreneur, you cannot just talk the talk and not walk the walk. You have to stand by your words firmly. Things will not happen unless you take actions on what you say. Being an entrepreneur teaches you that things do not happen as you have planned them, rather you have to get up and do them by yourself. Only actions will help bring your ideas to life.

**You Will Realize That There Are So Many Talented Ambitious People**

Being an entrepreneur can mean being lonely at times. It is useful to make friends with other entrepreneurs in your community or even around the world. You will eventually realize that there are so many people with different ambitions. You will also realize that you are not alone.

These entrepreneurs would be more than happy to share their experiences and thoughts with you. They may even give you the best advice and recommendations. There is an entire world out there that is yet to be discovered. As you unfold that world, you will learn and grow. The more you are immersed in the world of entrepreneurship, the more opportunities come to you, and the more driven you become.

**You Will Never Doubt Yourself Again**

By the time you take the leap of faith and gather the guts to start your own business, you would have already gotten rid of the doubts within you. While you will be working on developing your business, you will firmly believe in the quote, *"whatever you think you can do, or you can't, you're right."*

**You Will Want To Do It All Over Again**

There may be days when you might have succeeded or when you may have failed. Either way, you have learned so much in life that it makes it all worth the while. Starting something of your own gives you a sense of control in your life as well as the joy and fulfillment of doing something that you truly love.

All the stages that you have gone through, the rush, the excitement, the fear, the tears, the sweat and the countless nights, all are experiences that you will never forget.[1]

Now that we are aware of why starting a business is the best idea, let us look at the major benefits that a business can offer to its owner.

# Benefits of Owning Your Own Business

You may go through the bad days where you contemplate over the idea of starting your business in the first place. If you go through such days, the best way to tackle them is by revisiting the benefits of owning a business.

### You Are in Control

Being your own boss is a pretty great feeling. You do not have anyone to tell you what to do, and you have the choice to make the necessary decisions.

---

1 Huffpost (2019). *10 Reasons Why You Should Start Your Own Business.* Retrieved from https://www.huffpost.com/entry/10-reasons-why-you-should-start-your-own-business_b_8046036

### You Get to Build Something

That feeling you get when you have the power to create something is incomparable. When you own your business, you get the chance to shape your dreams.

### You Get to Help People

According to a survey, 96% of small business owners say that being able to help their customers is the major benefit of owning a business. These businesses also help people in creating jobs in their communities and contributing as community citizens.

### You Have the Option of a More Flexible Lifestyle

Owning your own business gives you the lifestyle flexibility you need to raise a family yet have a successful career. Women have benefited from this more as compared to men, but it is not only women. People who are close to being retired or are already retired find that owning a business gives them the chance to keep themselves busy and do something satisfying.

## You Might Change the World

Examples of Bill Gates and Mark Zuckerberg are few of those whose businesses have changed the world. Your business could be the next to bring a change globally. It may seem like a pretty ambitious target; however, nothing is impossible. Changing a piece for the better of the environment is a step towards changing the world.

## You Might Make More Money

Some businesses make a lot of money, whereas some don't. Most businesses provide their owners with a living and not a fortune. Regardless of the case, the point is that owning your business opens up a number of possibilities to make more money than you can while working as an employee.

Working as an employee can only give you a fixed wage, whereas running a business will earn you a significant amount of profit. There are more opportunities in making money in businesses as compared to just working. A number of other benefits are included along with the ones mentioned above. However, those who run a retail business may find it difficult to create a flexible lifestyle due to the demands of the retail trade. However, people who are self-employed rather than employed by someone else have more potential advantages. They are able to enjoy income tax breaks that are not available to the employees, such as hiring other family members and splitting the income. They are also able to work from home. On top of that, having your own business will let you wake up with a smile on a Monday morning instead of having to drag yourself forcefully to do a 9-5 job.[2]

With all the information provided above, it is pretty clear that starting your own business is one of the wisest decisions that you can make due to the number of benefits it gives and the satisfaction of life that it offers. The ease of working under your own conditions and being your own boss is a feeling that no 9-5 job can ever offer.

---

2The Balance (2019). *The Benefits of Owning Your Own Business.* Retrieved from https://www.thebalancesmb.com/the-advantages-of-owning-your-own-business-2948555

# Chapter 2
# Don't Be Afraid

Starting a business is meant to be really exciting, highly rewarding, and even challenging. With your own business, you get to be your own boss. You get to set your own direction and pursue all the opportunities that you are interested in. Your own business gives you the opportunity to work from home, in your pajamas with a cup of coffee in your hand, at any time of the day you feel comfortable.

However, not everyone is able to pursue the path of entrepreneurship. There are many reasons for this, some of which are:

## Inadequate Resources to Start a Business

Some people let go of the idea of starting their own business because they do not know where to find the capital they need. They are not sure of where to find the investors and how to get the investment for their business. They only rely on savings and do not have any rich family and friends to borrow from. These people are also worried that they will not pass the banks' lending criteria. Therefore, even if they want to start a business, the lack of money becomes a roadblock for them.

# No Knowledge of Entrepreneurship

People who let go of their plan to start a new business is also because they have never been exposed to entrepreneurship. Therefore, they have never considered business to be an option for them. Almost everyone in the world has worked jobs. That is why people are programmed to think that being an employee is the only path to earn money. Many entrepreneurs mostly have parents or relatives who have their own businesses, which inspires them to do the same and pursue their paths of entrepreneurship.

# Do Not Want the Stress of Entrepreneurship

Running a business is very stressful. This includes understanding the market, developing the right products and marketing properly in the right market. To run a business properly, the entrepreneur needs to possess the skills that are needed to run the business. These activities can become really challenging and stressful. Some people give up their dream of becoming an entrepreneur as they do not want to deal with the stress that comes with it.

## Passion for their Jobs

Some people choose not to pursue business because they are more passionate about their jobs. They love their current jobs, and they do not choose to do anything except that. They feel that the corporate world is already giving them a challenging and exciting environment that they crave for. Therefore, there is no reason for them to resign and pursue business.

## Fear

Starting a business means taking a huge risk since there is a possibility that it may work or may not work. Many people are scared of starting their own business because they fear that their business may not succeed. This fear may be due to feelings of inadequacy, or because they have experienced past failures in their lives that they do not want to go through the same process all over again. They may also be scared of competition and may be surrounded by people who, themselves, have self-doubts.[3]

# Fears Holding You Back From Starting a Business

We currently live in a world where a business can start from your couch at 3 AM with the help of free social media marketing and website templates. There can never be a better and easier time to start a business. That being said, a lot of people are still not able to become entrepreneurs.

People come up with excuses like, *"it's not the right time"*, *"we do not have enough money yet"* or *"we have a lot of responsibilities"*, etc. However, deep down, they know they are just making excuses. So what exactly are the fears that are holding down people from becoming entrepreneurs?

### It is Not the Right Time

Timing is an age-old excuse that we all use to get out of things that scare us. If all of us wait for the right time, we

---

3  PowerHomeBiz.com (2019). *12 Common Reasons Why People Don't Start Their Own Businesses.* Retrieved from https://www.powerhomebiz.com/starting-a-business/entrepreneurship/12-common-reasons-people-dont-start-businesses.htm

would be waiting forever. If you ever catch yourself using this phrase, then you need to stop and analyze what is really scaring you.

## What if I Fail?

Failure is an inevitable part of life, and it is one of the most terrifying aspects of starting a business. When you start developing a fear of failure, make a list of all the efforts that you have made to launch your startup. Once you conduct the research, you would come to know whether or not the product will work. All you need to do is trust yourself and take the risk. Yes, failure is always there, but even success is always present there. All you have to do is focus on the prize.

## You're Scared of Losing Stability

You have a 9-5 career. It may be a drag sometimes yet you have the control of it. You live for the weekends, and you are aware of when, where, and how you work. You get a stable paycheck, and you have a comfortable schedule. You may be scared of not earning on some days. However, you still have the feeling that if you do not take the leap now, you may just never have the guts to move forward and leave.

## Everything Isn't Perfect

So you have your plan all set. You have learned your business plan by heart, and you know exactly how you want it to turn out. But then the inevitable happens. Something just has to go wrong. Things change. Your investor is not as excited as he was when he first heard of your business plan. Or it could be possible that your website designer did not exactly portray what you imagined and you do not have the money to revise it anymore. Your marketing plan requires more money than you thought it would. Don't panic. Stop. Breathe.

Many young entrepreneurs get it wrong the first time. It's okay. Everyone has dreams. All you have to do is be realistic. You cannot give up just because your website did not have the color scheme you wanted. You need to find solutions and apply them to the problems. The truth is, starting a business is a really daunting step. However, if you are not scared, then you are definitely doing something wrong. Fear is the first step to success and fear is what drives us to make the best decisions.[4]

---

4 Due Inc. (2019). *4 Fears Holding You Back From Starting A Business.* Retrieved from https://due.com/blog/4-fears-holding-back-starting-business/

# Why People Fear Starting a Business?

The above-mentioned points are the reasons as to why we do not take our decisions of starting a business seriously. However, while some people succeed in overcoming those reasons, many other external factors arise due to which people opt to play it safe and erase their business plans. Some of those external factors are:

### The Economy

One major external factor that causes people to let go of their business plan is how the economy is doing. If the economy is really low, many entrepreneurs would perceive that it is not a good time to start a business. This belief has been reinforced by politicians and journalists who emphasize and exaggerate the news.

However, the fact is that there is no single thing that is called 'the economy'. The economy is a vast, interconnected web of buyers and sellers that work together through a market and price system. Also, there are two sides to every transaction. One side of the economy may be hurting while the other side may be thriving.

## Uncertainty

Another fear that stops the entrepreneurs from pursuing their business is the uncertainty that comes with owning a business. Business ownership does not provide immediate or guaranteed pay. The income depends on the sales and profits of the company. If you are someone who is used to being paid on a regular schedule, then jumping starting a business may seem really difficult at first. It is completely acceptable to worry if your business will be enough to provide for you or your family.

There is an opposite side to uncertainty. When your business helps you generate an income, you are solely entitled to it. No boss or employer can take it away. You will not have to plead for a raise or demonstrate and prove why you deserve more. In a business, your income depends entirely on what you produce and sell.

## Indecision

Some people are afraid to start their own business because they are indecisive of what type of business they should start. These people want to be self-employed, but they don't know in what capacity. To start a business, one needs to have the necessary skills and knowledge in that particular field of business. One can refer to previous jobs. For example, in a previous job if one was an accountant, maybe he can start his own accounting firm. Changing course and getting into a completely new field is a huge risk.

## Debt

Debt is a serious reason to consider when opting for entrepreneurship. If you are one who is burdened with student loans or credit card bills, then it is difficult to get the required start-up finance. There may be chances that the income your business generates may end up going to the creditors.

Debt is a major and a completely justifiable reason to fear when starting a business. The best way to handle it is to clear yourself of any debts and then move towards your business with a clear mind.

## Family Obligations

Financial concerns are not the only reason to reconsider the decision of starting a business. The early days of a new business venture can be incredibly taxing, and people fear not spending much time with their families. Having a recently established business, you will end up giving 10-12 hours of your day at work. At the end of the day, you will be left with no spare time to give to your family.

However, one can always discuss the situation with their spouse and decide over what arrangements and sacrifices need to be made during the early days of the company.

## No Benefits

Every entrepreneur fears about losing benefits of a good job such as health insurance or 401(k) contributions. However, not every situation is like that. Different retirement accounts can be opened and funded without the help of an employer.[5]

In the USA, a survey identified that 57% of people have at least one idea for a business. However, only two-fifths actually take the leap and implement it. There will always be uncertainty when one starts his own business. Vulnerability and questioning come with every decision that one makes in

---

5  Grasshopper (2019). *6 Reasons Why People Are Afraid to Start a Business.* retrieved from https://grasshopper.com/blog/6-reasons-why-people-are-afraid-to-start-a-business/

life. But what separates achieving the dream from only sitting on the sidelines is the ability to jump and take the leap.[6]

# Finding Business Opportunities and Making it Happen

*"Failure is simply the opportunity to begin again, this time more intelligently."*

**-Henry Ford**

The creator of the first mass-produced automobile was very certain of what he was talking about. Henry Ford knew about all the opportunities, and he made use of all of them. Till this day, opportunities stand against the tests of all time.

A business opportunity is defined as having the chance to be able to meet a market's need, interest or want through a creative combination of resources. This is exactly what an entrepreneur needs in order to survive in the business world. However, identifying those resources and acting on them is

---

6  Entrepreneur (2019). *How to Conquer Your Fear of Starting a Business.* retrieved from https://www.entrepreneur.com/article/302154

not as easy as it sounds. There are different tips and tricks to attain these resources and pave your way through success.

### Think Outside the Box

Although this may sound like a very old saying, it can be effectively applied and can be the key to success. You have to look for opportunities that others may have missed. Finding that point and creating a corresponding innovative solution is what will keep your business ahead of the game.

### Know What is Inside the Box

In order to think outside the box, you need to know what is inside the box. This means learning and knowing about your competitors. You need to know anything and everything about the industry you are about to step in. This means past, present, and predictions for the future. When you know what is available and what might be available, then you can come up with something that is truly innovative to fill the market gap.

## Have Confidence

Once you have done your homework and have all the insights about your specific field, it is important that you take advantage of an opportunity even if you doubt its success. Innovation does not come from certain outcomes, but it comes from taking risks and trying new things. Taking the jump will be scary, but the more knowledge and experience you have, the easier it becomes.

## Do What Others Do Not Want To

Search for the things that other businesses are not doing. The reason may be because they are time-consuming, dirty or boring. However, these jobs still need to be done. All you need to do is take a bullet and offer these services. You may be just transforming a want into a need.

## Ask for More Than You Think You Will Get

Lastly, do not be afraid to aim higher than you currently are. You just might be surprised by the outcome.[7]

---

7 PowWowNow (2019). *How to Spot (and act on) New Business Opportunities.* Retrieved from https://www.powwownow.co.uk/smarter-working/spot-act-business-opportunities

## Embrace Your Mistakes

As mentioned earlier, failure is inevitable. You can never avoid it. It has to happen at some point or the other. When you are establishing a business, many people will come up to you and offer you all kinds of advice. But one advice that you may not hear very often is: *"Make lots of mistakes"*.

What do potato chips, post-it notes, pacemakers, and penicillin have in common? They were started by making mistakes. In each of these cases, the inventor attempted to create something completely different and failed. What they did not realize was that they had actually come up with an innovative new product.

Failures, mishaps, and mistakes all play an important role in helping the employees learn and grow. However, organizations do not let us make mistakes. Employees are penalized if they do so. This is why they end up being too shy or nervous to try something new.

If you are not failing, then you are probably not winning either. Despite sounding counter-intuitive, this is the most important point. Think about it; if everything you are doing is working out, then it means you are not taking enough risks and are simply playing safe. You are not challenging yourself to achieve big goals that will separate you from the rest. You probably are not learning more than what you already know. Everyone cannot know everything. There is always something more to learn about, and that is why entrepreneurs always seek for new perspectives that challenge them. With more knowledge, they are able to make better decisions for the business when everyone is encouraged to bring their unique ideas on the table.[8]

By feeling stifled or scared to make mistakes, the organization will not be able to reap those benefits. You need to encourage yourself to fail and accept all the benefits that come from making the mistakes.[9]

---

8  Entrepreneur (2019). *Why Embracing Failure is Good for Business.* Retrieved from https://www.entrepreneur.com/article/315384
9  Ladders (2019). *Why Making Mistakes is Actually Good for Business.* Retrieved from https://www.theladders.com/career-advice/why-making-mistakes-is-actually-good-for-business

# Chapter 3
# Legal Entity

As an entrepreneur, who is just starting a new venture, there are many things going on that are keeping you busy. These things may include activities like developing products, getting users or hiring new employees. Not a lot of startup companies worry about the legal aspects of their business at an early stage, and some of them even form a legal entity of the business much later. It is understandable to wait and know whether or not your company needs a legal entity before actually forming one.[10]

Launching a startup takes a lot of courage, vision, creativity, and determination. You will have to align your business model to the needs of the market, find the right staff to execute your plans, manufacture high-quality products, invest in marketing and set up a corporate network that can boost growth and revenue of the company. Throughout this process, it is easy to lose sight of the fact that a startup is

---

10 Law Trades (2019). *When Is It Necessary to Create a Legal Entity for a Startup?* Retrieved from https://www.lawtrades.com/answers/necessary-create-legal-entity-startup/

nothing but a legal entity and all legal entities need professional support.[11]

## What is a Legal Entity?

A legal entity discusses a legally standing or a lawful partnership. The partnership can be anything from an association, a trust, a proprietorship, a corporation or even an individual. All these entities are legally capable of being accountable for certain activities against the law, enter contracts or agreements, incur and pay back debts, be sued and sue other entities, and even assume obligations. Legal entities are able to do a lot of things.

However, a legal entity cannot hold office or cast a vote. Legal entities are seen in scenarios and situations where an individual can take a class-action lawsuit against a company or even a manufacturer that supplies the products for a company.[12] Once you have your business plan ready to be executed, you can now work on keeping your company safe.

11 Young Upstarts (2019). *How Important is the Legal Department for a Startup Company?* Retrieved from http://www.youngupstarts.com/2018/06/28/how-important-is-the-legal-department-for-a-startup-company/
12 Upcounsel (2019). *Legal Entity: Everything You Need to Know.* Retrieved from https://www.upcounsel.com/legal-entity

Practicing some caution and taking proper legal steps to secure your business and your personal interests will help you avoid any pitfalls that may come your way.

Some ways to secure your business may include:

**Safeguard your Interests**

You do not want to let your ideas out of the bag and into the world, especially if you fear that your competitors may benefit from them. Neither do you want your employees to do so. To protect your intellectual property assets like trademarks, patents, and trade secrets, make your employees, contractors, consultants and business partners sign a Confidential Information and Invention Assignment Agreement. This agreement states that all the intellectual property created or disclosed by the company remains the property of the company.

If you have an invention and you want to protect it, apply for a Provisional Patent. This lets you use a *"patent pending"* notice to keep others from copying your invention while you are working on starting your startup.

You can also include a non-compete clause in an Employment Agreement that prohibits an employee from competing against you or solicit your employees or customers for a limited time after leaving your company.

## Set Up a Legal Entity

The next step is to decide on which type of legal entity formation is best for your business. Some of the Legal Structures include:

- Sole Proprietorship

- Partnership

- Limited Liability Company (LLC)

- Corporation[13]

When starting a business, it is important to safeguard yourself. Take small initiatives such as opening your own mail so you can track your finances yourself, making sure that you are the first person to see any complaints or new business opportunities. Make sure to use passwords and other computer security steps. Avoid storing sensitive

---

13    Rocket Lawyer (2019). *A Legal Guide for Startups.* Retrieved from https://www.rocketlawyer.com/article/a-legal-guide-for-startups.rl

financial data online. Share your financial data only with your accountant and your lawyer but make sure to limit to those who can see it.

## Sole Proprietorship

A sole proprietorship is also known as a sole trader or a proprietorship. It is an unincorporated business that has only one owner who pays the personal income tax on the profits earned from the business.

A sole proprietorship is the easiest type of business because of the few government regulations as compared to other forms of partnerships. As such, sole proprietorship's are very popular among individual self-contractors, consultants or small business owners. Many sole proprietors do business under their names because creating a separate business name is not required.

A sole proprietorship is very different from corporations and limited partnerships because no separate legal identity is created. As a result, the business owner of a sole proprietorship is not exempted from liabilities that are incurred by the entity.

For example, the debts of the sole proprietorship are also debts of the owner. However, the profits of the sole proprietorship are also the profits of the owner because all profits directly flow to him/her.

One of the main benefits of a sole proprietorship is the pass-through tax advantage. One of the disadvantages is in getting capital funding, specifically through established channels, like issuing equity and obtaining bank loans or lines of credit. As a business grows, it transitions to a limited liability company (LLC) or an S-corporation.

Usually, when a sole proprietor seeks to incorporate a business, the owner restructures it and turns it into an LLC. For this to work, the owner has to determine if the name of the company is available and if it is, the articles of the organization must be filed with the state office where the business will be based.

After the paperwork has been completed, the business owner needs to create an LLC opening agreement which clearly states the business structure. Lastly, an Employment Identification Number (EIN) is allotted to the business.[14]

---

14 Investopedia (2019). *Sole Proprietorship.* Retrieved from

# Partnership

A partnership is a formal arrangement by two or more parties to operate a business and share its profits. There are many different types of partnership arrangements. In some partnerships, all partners share liabilities and profits equally, whereas, in others, partners have limited liability. There is also a partner called the *"silent partner"*, in which one party has no concern about the day-to-day operations of the business.

A partnership can be any endeavor that is undertaken jointly by a number of different parties. The parties can be governments, non-profit enterprises, businesses or even private individuals. Even the goals of partnership vary. There are three main categories of partnerships. The general partnership, the limited partnership, and the limited liability limited partnership.

- In general partnership, all parties share the legal and financial liability equally. The individuals are responsible for the debts that the partnership takes on. Profits are

---

https://www.investopedia.com/terms/s/soleproprietorship.asp

shared equally. All the details regarding the sharing are mentioned in writing on a partnership agreement.

- Limited liability partnerships are a common structure for professionals like accountants, lawyers, and architects. This arrangement limits the partners' personal liability. So if one partner is sued for malpractice, the assets of the other partner are not at risk.

- Limited partnerships are a hybrid of general partnerships and limited liability partnerships. In a limited partnership, at least one partner must be a general partner with full personal liability for the partnership's debts. Whereas, there is one partner who is a silent partner whose liability is limited to the amount invested. This silent partner does not participate in the management nor in the day-to-day operations of the partnership.

- Lastly, the limited liability limited partnership is a new and relatively uncommon kind. This limited partnership provides greater protection from liability for its general partners.

These basic varieties of partnerships can be found throughout common law jurisdictions. However, there are differences depending on the laws governing them in each jurisdiction. In regards to taxes, there is no federal statute defining partnerships. Nevertheless, the Internal Revenue Code includes detailed rules on their federal tax treatment. Partnerships do not pay income tax. The tax responsibility passes through to the partners. These partners are also not considered employees for tax purposes. Individuals who are in partnerships may receive more favorable tax treatment than if they had founded a corporation. That means corporate profits are taxed just like the dividends paid to owners or shareholders. On the other hand, partnerships' profits are not double-taxed in this manner.[15]

# Limited Liability Company (LLC)

A limited liability company (LLC) is a corporate structure in the United States where the owners are not personally liable for the company's debts or liabilities. Limited liability companies are hybrid entities that are a combination of the characteristics of a corporation with those of a partnership or sole proprietorship. Limited liability companies (LLCs) are allowed under state statutes. The regulations that are surrounding LLCs differ from state to state. LLC owners are

---

15 Investopedia (2019). *Partnership.* Retrieved from
https://www.investopedia.com/terms/p/partnership.asp

generally compared to the members. Many states do not restrict ownership which means that anyone can be a member such as individuals, corporations, foreigners and foreign entities, and also other LLCs. There are also some entities that cannot form LLCs, including banks and insurance companies.

An LLC is a more formal partnership arrangement which requires articles of organization to be filed with the state. It is much easier to form an LLC as compared to a corporation as well as it provides more flexibility and protection. LLCs do not pay taxes themselves. Instead, profits and losses are listed on the personal tax returns of the owner.

The primary reason business owners choose to go down the LLC route is because they can limit the principals' personal liability. Many look at LLC as a blend of a partnership, which is a simple business formation of two or more owners in an agreement, and a corporation which has certain liability protections. LLCs have some attractive features, and they also have several disadvantages.

Depending on the law of the state, an LLC may have to be dissolved upon the death of a partner, or the bankruptcy of a partner. An LLC may not be a suitable option when the ultimate objective of the founder is to become a publicly-traded company.[16]

# Corporation

A corporation is a legal entity that is separate and distinct from its owners. Corporations enjoy the rights and responsibilities that an individual possesses, such as enter contracts, loan and borrow money, sue and be sued, hire employees, own assets, and pay taxes.

All businesses around the globe use corporations. Its legal status may vary from jurisdiction to jurisdiction. However, a corporation's most important aspect is a limited liability. This means that the shareholders get a chance to take part in the profits through dividends and stock appreciation. Nonetheless, they are not liable for the company's debts.

A corporation is created when it is incorporated by a group of shareholders who have the ownership of the corporation, represented by their holding of common stock, and with the aim to pursue a common goal. The goals of a

---

16       Investopedia (2019). *Limited Liability Company (LLC).* Retrieved from https://www.investopedia.com/terms/l/llc.asp

corporation can be for profit or not for profit. However, the majority of corporations aim to provide a return for their shareholders.

Shareholders are only responsible for the payment of their shares to the company's treasury upon issuance. A corporation may have a single shareholder or several. With publicly traded corporations, there are thousands of shareholders.

## Operations of a Corporation

The shareholders annually elect a board of directors that appoints and oversees the management of the corporation and its day-to-day activities. The board of directors then executes the corporation's business plan and must take all the means to do so. Although the members of the board are not responsible for the debts of the corporation, yet it is their duty to maintain the well-being of the corporation.

When the corporation achieves its objectives, its legal life can be terminated through a process known as liquidation. For this process, a company appoints a liquidator who sells the corporation's assets, then the company pays any creditors and gives any remaining assets back to the shareholders. The process of liquidation can be voluntary or even involuntary. If it is involuntary, the creditors of an insolvent corporation usually trigger it, and that may lead to the bankruptcy of the corporation.[17]

# Other Legal Documentation Required for Business

Documents play an important role in protecting the interests of the business and the business owners over the course of time. Some of the common legal documents include:

### Company Bylaws for Corporations

Most of the states require corporations to keep a written record of the bylaws. However, one may not need to file the document with a state office. Bylaws define how the company will govern itself. Even if the company is incorporated in the states that do not require bylaws, they are

---

17 Investopedia (2019). *Corporation.* Retrieved from
https://www.investopedia.com/terms/c/corporation.asp

still a good idea because they define the structure of the business, the individual roles, and the governance issues.

**Meeting Minutes**

Many states also require corporations to document what happens during major meetings. They keep an official account of what was done or talked about in the meetings, including any decisions made or any actions taken. They can help in settling a dispute about what exactly happened or didn't happen in the past meeting.

The minutes should be detailed enough to serve as the corporation's *"institutional memory"*. They should include details like the type of meeting, time and place of meeting, detailed attendance, all actions taken, and any votes including how everyone voted and who abstained.

**Operating Agreement for LLCs**

Most states do not require it, yet an operating agreement is recommended for every LLC; especially when there are many members involved. This document outlines an LLC's financial and functional decisions. If there is more than one member, it becomes imperative to define how the business decisions will be made, how the profits and losses will be calculated, what are the rights and obligations of each member, and what happens when someone wants to exit. Once the members sign the document, it becomes an official, binding contract.

## Non-disclosure Agreement

Every business has information that should remain private such as customers' list, financial records or ideas for a new pricing plan. An NDA is the first line of defense to protect such information. This legal document creates a confidential relationship between your business and any contractors, employees or other business partners who might want to get a behind-the-scenes look at your operations.

## Employment Agreement

This contract sets the rules, obligations, and expectations of the company and the employee to reduce any future disputes. Not every person hired requires an employment agreement. The document can come in handy if you want to discourage new hires from leaving the company, disclosing confidential information about the business or work with a competitor. The contract needs to be reviewed by an experienced employment law attorney before it is given to an employee for signature.

## Business Plan

A business plan may not be a legal document; however, it is required if the company ever decides on seeking financing or selling the business. The business plan can be of one page, or it can be of a hundred pages, as long as it provides the clarity on your business' opportunity and your roadmap to get there.

## Memorandum of Understanding

An MOU is something that falls between a formal contract and a handshake. It records any important conversations that you have with suppliers, potential suppliers and others that are involved in the business. MOUs are a great way to lay out the terms of a project or a relationship in writing, but they do not rely on the document to be legally binding.

## Online Terms of Use

This may not be required by the law; however, any business that has a website should include their terms of use. These pages can limit your liability in cases where there are errors present in your content, as well as information contained in the hyperlinks from your website. Also, your terms should let the visitors know what they can or cannot do on your site, especially in cases where the visitors can comment on blogs or share their own content.

## Online Privacy Policy

If you gather any information from your customers or website visitors, you are legally required to post a privacy policy that states how the information you have gathered will be or not be used.

## Apostille

Businesses that are involved in international trade with other Hague Convention countries may require a certificate which is known as *"apostille"*. This authenticates the origin of a public document so they can be recognized in another country. Apostilles are valid only in countries that are members of the Hague Convention. You may not need to create these documents from scratch. You can simply find templates available    online to serve as an idea. These legal documents    are important to stay compliant with your state requirements. However, they are more than just empty formalities. By taking the time to think about the various elements on each document, you are practically setting the right foundation for your business.[18]

---

18        Entrepreneur (2019). *The 10 Key Legal Documents for Your Business*. Retrieved from https://www.entrepreneur.com/article/236967

# Chapter 4
# Location

The positioning of a business has always been the basic and the most important element in setting up a business. The success of your business depends on how well you are positioned in the market, so you are easily found. Positioning includes a number of different factors that begin with location to pricing to promoting your business, online or offline.

There is a famous piece of advice, *"Location, Location, Location"*. This is how important location is when we talk about business. Despite the rise of technology, virtual communication, and the cloud, it is important for a business to have a business address.

If the address of your business is far away from your specific target audience, the prospective clients may find it difficult to locate and reach you. In the same way, if you have a city center location or if you are located in an area, which is regarded as a business center, in that case, the prospective clients will be more inclined to do business with you.

# How Important is Location to your Business?

### The Best Location Can Increase Brand Visibility

The location has an impact on many different factors, such as:

- The ability of the business to market itself

- The competition it faces from other businesses

- The total cost of operation

- The taxes the business owner has to pay

- The regulations they have to follow

The location also matters when marketing. The importance of location goes beyond just the physical location of the business and the website rank in Google searches. It has an impact on the placement of your advertisements.

## Easy Access is a Huge Advantage

You want to be wherever your customers are and make it as convenient for them as possible. Location is important for a business that sells goods or services directly to customers at brick and mortar establishments.

Some customers even choose to buy from specific companies because of the image they have about those companies in their heads. A business located in the commercial area of the city gives the perception that the business is successful and can afford to be located at a prime location.

Your business also needs to consider if there is parking space for prospective customers. Many customers will prefer going somewhere else if it is too hard to find a parking space.

## Consider your Suppliers

Depending on your type of business, suppliers can influence your choice of location. Price and quality are pre-requisites in choosing a supplier. However, the speed of delivery has a huge impact on productivity. For better and quicker business operations, it is necessary to consider the location of your company to make it easier for your suppliers to reach your location on time in order to deliver goods and provide services required for your business to run smoothly. The closer you are located to your suppliers, the quicker your product can be sold to the market.

The location will always be important for all businesses despite the rise of remote work, collaboration, telecommuting, and virtual offices. If your business is located in a convenient location to attract customers, you can be certain of growth, an increase in sales, and brand visibility.

If you are operating your business in a traditional way, which is having only a physical presence, then your success mostly depends on your location. Therefore, you need to choose your location carefully.[19]

**Competition**

The location of a business can affect the competition that your business faces from businesses that sell similar products and services. For example, an upscale

---

19    Alltopstartups (2018). *The Importance of Location in Business.* Retrieved from https://alltopstartups.com/2018/03/15/the-importance-of-location-in-business/

neighborhood will have dozens of restaurants. A small town, on the other hand, will not have any businesses that sell ethnic food. Therefore, starting a business in an area with few direct competitors can increase the likelihood of attracting customers.

**Operating Expenses**

The location of a business can have a huge impact on the total cost of operations. Renting a storefront on a popular and high-end street or mall will be more expensive as compared to a store in a small commercial district in a residential area. A business will be better off opening its doors in an area that is cheap even if it gives you few sales.

**Taxes and Regulations**

The location of a business determines the state and the local taxes that owners have to pay and the rules that they need to follow. Income tax and sales tax rates vary from one area to another. They have a significant impact on the earnings of the business owner. The government has zoning laws that limit the size and construction of the buildings and the excessive usage of signboards. The state and local laws can also have an effect on the type of permits and licenses necessary to operate a business.[20]

## Types of Business and Their Locations

If you are a retail business or if you are a manufacturer of a product and distribution is a vital element of your business operations, then geographical location is very important. If you have a business that is information or service-related, the actual location takes a back seat to whether or not the facility itself can meet your needs.

Regardless of the nature of your business, before you start shopping for space, you need to have a clear picture of what you need to have, what you would like to have, what you will not tolerate, and how much you can pay for it.

Creating that picture is a time-consuming, exciting and a tedious process. However, it is essential for you to pay attention to it. Many startup decisions can be corrected with time, but a poor choice of location is a difficult decision to change, and sometimes it becomes impossible to repair. The

---

20     Azcentral.com (2019). *Why is Business Location Important?* Retrieved from https://yourbusiness.azcentral.com/business-location-important-3566.html

type of location you choose depends largely on the type of business that you are in; however, there are enough areas that can be used in many different ways. You should give a thought to each type of location space before making the final decision.

For example, business parks and office buildings have retail space so that they are able to attract restaurants and stores that business owners are looking for nearby. Shopping centers are usually for different professional services like medical, legal, accounting, insurance companies, etc. You can practically use any nontraditional space and make it work for you. All you need to do is use your imagination.

## Home Based Business

This is the trendiest location for a business these days, and many entrepreneurs start in the premises of their home. They then move to a commercial location as their business grows. Some entrepreneurs even start their businesses at home with no intention of moving. A home-based business can be run from an office space in a spare bedroom, the basement, the attic or even the kitchen table. On a positive note, you do not need to worry about negotiating the leases that come up with significant deposits. On the negative side, you have a very limited room for growth, and it may be a challenge for you to accommodate employees or meet your clients.

# Retail Business

Retail space comes in a variety of different shapes and sizes, and it can be located in different malls, strip shopping centers, free-standing buildings, downtown shopping districts or mixed-use facilities. You can also find different retail spaces in airports and other transportation facilities, hotel lobbies, sports stadiums and a variety of temporary or special event venues.

## Mall Space

A mall consists of many retailers that are competing with each other under one roof. In a mall, there are usually 3 to 5 anchor stores or large chain stores and dozens of smaller retail shops. Due to the high customer traffic in malls, the rent of stores in malls is higher as compared to other retail locations. Before you select this type of store location, you need to make sure that the mall shopper demographic matches that of your customers. Mall retailers have to sacrifice a lot of independence and have to follow a set of rules that have been specified by the mall management.

**Shopping Center**

Strip malls and other adjoining retail locations also have a set of rules and guidelines of how they want their tenants to run their business. These rules are lesser as compared to that of a mall. Some shopping centers may have as few as 3 units or as many as 20. The types of retailers and the type of goods or services will vary. One important element to investigate is the parking area for your customers.

**Downtown Area**

Just like the mall, this type of store location is another premium choice. However, there may be more freedom and fewer rules for the business owner. Many communities work hard to revive their downtown areas, while retailers can take advantage of such opportunities. However, there is one issue in this case, and that is the lack of parking.

### Free Standing Locations

This type of retail location is just any stand-alone building. It can be tucked away in a neighborhood location or right off a busy highway. It depends on the landlord. There are no restrictions on how a retailer should operate his business.

Freestanding locations have a good space for parking, and the cost per square foot is also reasonable. Unlike the attached retail locations, the retailer of a free-standing location has to market the business in order to grab the customers.[21]

# Mobile

Whether your business is meant to cater to the general public or other businesses, if you have a product or service that you take to your customers, then, in that case, your ideal location may be a car, van or a truck. Examples of business that are mobile can be pet grooming services, food truck, party transportation, tutoring, auto detailing, personal

---

21 The Balance (2019). *The Different Types of Retail Locations.* Retrieved from https://www.thebalancesmb.com/types-of-retail-locations-2890244

trainer, cleaning services, etc.

# Commercial

Commercial space includes more options as compared to retail. Commercial office buildings and business parks offer traditional office space that is geared into businesses that do not require a significant amount of pedestrian or automobile traffic for sales.

Office space can be found in downtown business districts, business parks, and sometimes interspersed among suburban retail facilities. One office option to consider is an executive suite, where the landlord provides receptionist and secretarial services, faxing, photocopying, conference rooms, and other support services as part of the space package.

Executive suites help you in projecting the image of a professional operation at a more affordable cost than a traditional office. They can be found in most commercial areas. Some executive suites even rent their facilities by the hour to home-based businesses or to people who are from out of town who need a temporary office space.

**Office**

From downtown high rises to suburban office malls, the office spaces available are usually large in size within the commercial real estate. Though much of the volume is in leasing when a sale takes place, yet the size isn't affected as much. A firm that understands the needs of the lease client in their business goes a long way in being successful as a commercial real estate agent in the office space.

Dealing with the local and national business requires a firm grip on the characteristics of the market. Repeat business in larger areas can make this a well-paid commercial real estate specialty.

When leasing a commercial space, you need to consider whether your business has frequent clients coming or not. If not, then a commercial space is the place you need.

The next thing you need to consider is if your business requires space. Does it thrive off people who are coming in throughout the day and making a purchase, or scheduling a service? Or is your business more of an office setting where clients communicate through email or a phone call throughout the day? If it's yes to the first question, then office space is definitely what you require.[22]

## Industrial

If your business is the kind that involves manufacturing or heavy distribution, you will need a plant or warehouse facility. Light industrial parks attract smaller manufacturers in nonpolluting industries as well as companies that need showrooms in addition to the manufacturing facilities.

Industrial areas tend to be older and poorly planned, and usually, they offer rail and water port access. Industrial parks are newer, and they have better infrastructures. Therefore, you may want to consider any free-standing commercial building that meets your needs and is adequately zoned.[23]

## Manufacturing Facilities

Simply put, manufacturing facilities are sites where companies produce and assemble goods. There are a handful of common factors that are required in manufacturing

---

22 Rosetti Properties (2019). *Retail Space Vs. Commercial Space – What's The Difference?* Retrieved from https://www.rosettiproperties.com/rosetti-properties-news/retail-space-vs-commercial-space-what-s-the-difference
23 Entrepreneur (2019). *Choosing a Location for Your Business.* Retrieved from https://www.entrepreneur.com/article/21830

facilities, and there are many variations available. These differences revolve around the size of the equipment and the type/amount of materials used throughout the manufacturing process. Common uses of heavy industry sites include a number of refineries, utilities, meatpacking companies, semiconductor producers and other key industries. With the required specialized equipment, heavy industry space is not quickly interchangeable between companies.

However, light industry manufacturing sites are far more flexible, and they require significantly less square footage and customization. These facilities are used to assemble products that are manufactured somewhere else. After the products are assembled, these light industries store the products until they are ready to be shipped.


**Warehouse Space**

This space is defined as a planned space for efficient storage and the handling of goods and materials. The warehouse is a concept that has become more of a convergence between the traditional storage and the distribution centers.

The distribution warehouses function as a critical hub in the logistics network. Their location is very important as it allows them to serve a predetermined region efficiently. They work as part of an overall web of evenly spaced distribution facilities that coordinate with one another. When selecting a distribution warehouse space, the location is the most important. The space of the warehouse should be enough to effectively serve its customer base and make the overall process efficient via automated technologies.

Truck and railway terminals are a subset of the distribution centers, and they exist for the sole purpose of transferring the inventory from one truck, railcar, or shipping container to another. The terminals are intermediary sites and exclusively serve transportation purposes.

Another important kind of warehouse is the general warehousing. There is a huge demand for the space that meets the traditional ideas of warehousing, which is geared specifically for inventory storage.

The general warehouse differs from the other types of warehouses as it does not require countless rows of rolling doors or specialized machinery. The price of a general warehouse does not place a significant premium on proximity to transportation since agility is a secondary concern as compared to sufficient size and storage capacity.

**Flex Space**

A flex space is designed to provide flexibility to the tenant in its usage. This adaptability is important for small to mid-size companies that have a need for both office and warehouse space but do not have the budget nor the staff to support two separate leases and properties.

Since the spaces tend to be purposely plain in construction and are designed to maximize usefulness, price points are also lower in comparison to similar square footage in other types of industrial space.

The make use of the flex space, a company, can add or remove features to make the space fulfill their specific needs. This flexibility in space creates both operational and cost efficiencies by leveraging the square footage to serve more applications while requiring only one lease.

R&D facilities are a specialized version of flex space, which typically require lower ratios of office space to the total square footage. However, the usage varies from company to company. R&D requires laboratory testing in many different fields. Therefore, the space can also take the form of massive silos. Due to the highly digitized nature of modern commerce, most companies require some degree of data storage. This requires specific facilities to house the storage equipment, run IT systems, and facilitate cloud storage. For such activities, companies , their own facilities and space for climate control and security protocols.

Lastly, showrooms are an important type of flex space, which allow companies to showcase their products in a controlled environment. As businesses are evolving toward a more specialized approach to manufacturing, distribution, and sales, industrial space will eventually evolve with them. More and more advanced supply chains will only push industrial space further toward a greater number of categories and subsets in highly customizable facilities.[24] There are many options available for businesses that are starting out and are considering their business location choice.

---

24      Tenant Base (2019). *8 Types of Industrial & Warehouse Office Space.* Retrieved from https://blog.tenantbase.com/8-types-of-industrial-warehouse-office-space

There will be many cost implications and practical considerations to make with every location choice. If you choose to rent or buy premises, factor in the monthly mortgage or rent costs as well as any shared services in the building. Also, make sure that you have a complete picture of what that specific space will cost you.

Another simple option could be to use a shared space where you can take a desk space or a room in an existing office and share it with other businesses that are residing there. This process is known as *"hot desking"*, and it is a growing trend amongst businesses that aim to generate income. Therefore, you need to consider all the opportunities in the areas that suit your business.

If you have a small budget and you do not require a physical office location, you can always opt for a virtual office service depending on the company you buy from. There should be an official address with which you can register your business and include a mail forwarding option so you can have all your mails sent there. That being said, your business address says a lot about your business itself. Therefore, you need to take the time and get it right so you can benefit from it for years to come.[25]

---

25     Entrepreneur & Investor (2019). *The Importance of Location in Business*. Retrieved from http://entrepreneurandinvestor.com/the-importance-of-location-in-business/

# Chapter 5
# Gathering the Resources

Starting a business is a hard task; however, many people still seem to successfully run their businesses. Those who succeed spend a lot of their time in raising capital, doing market research, and developing a realistic business plan before launching their own company. This requires a lot of careful planning. It may not guarantee your success, but it can improve your chances enormously. All you need to do is make a log of your resources and be prepared to meet the challenges that may come your way.

The resources that a company may need can be broken down into five broad categories: financial, human, educational, emotional, and physical resources.

**Financial Resources**

The most important element in starting a business is funding. Even the most basic businesses that are home-based require startup costs, including registering a business name, obtaining a business telephone line, and printing business cards. Financial resources can be obtained from a number of different sources. The easiest source is getting it from the personal accounts of the owner of the company. Other sources include loans and lines of credit that may be granted from financial institutions, friends and relatives, private investors, and even the government. Also, many grants are offered from private and public sources to entrepreneurs of all demographics and personal situations.

## Human Resources

The success of an organization is heavily dependent on the talents and strengths of its employees. The hiring of these experienced professionals, who have records of excellence in their areas of expertise, makes sure that the mission and the goals of the company are carried out efficiently and with competence. Strong team members of an organization can be recruited through a number of different methods.

There are staffing agencies and executive firms that specialize in placing the right talent in the right positions of the industry. An alternative step is to find employees through referrals from individuals whose judgment is trusted.

## Educational Resources

The greatest thing that an entrepreneur can do when starting his own business is to gain as much education as possible. By understanding the competition and gaining an in-depth knowledge of the industry, the entrepreneur will be well-prepared to make smarter decisions for the company. Educational resources can be found through professional trade associations that are geared toward the industry, the local chamber of commerce, and the Small Business Administration.

## Physical Resources

Whether the business is conducted in a home or at a suite, every organization needs to have a proper physical resource in order to survive. This includes a proper workspace, working telephone line, sufficient information systems, and effective marketing materials. This part of business planning is one of the most expensive ones. However, it is important for an entrepreneur to assess his needs before he makes any actual purchases.

### Emotional Resources

Starting a business is a stressful journey for an entrepreneur. In order to maintain his sanity and stay motivated at the same time, it is important for the entrepreneur to have a proper support team that can inspire him and push him to keep moving on. This support team can comprise of friends, family, mentors or even a professional group.[26]

# Essential Equipment for Starting a Business

When you are starting a business or an office, you will require both office furniture and office equipment. Purchasing office equipment like computers, software, printers, fax machines, and network equipment will be your second largest expense. If you plan your expenses carefully, you will be able to control them by purchasing essential items needed to function.

---

[26]     Chron (2019). *5 Resources You Need to Succeed to Start a Business.* Retrieved from https://smallbusiness.chron.com/5-resources-need-succeed-start-business-23.html

### Business Telephone System

The primary means that you will be using to communicate with your customers and your vendors will be the telephone. Understanding what services, features, and options are available will help you in determining the right size of the phone for the right price for your business.

### Computers and Software

Information is the most vital element of any successful organization today. The key to leveraging information to your advantage is by purchasing and implementing the right computers and software for your business.

Also, you will have to explore different systems for the backup of your business data. There are many services available online that will save you from investing in a secure and reliable backup equipment for the office.

### Computer Network and Internet Connection

If the information is important, then so are computer networks. It is responsible for channeling information to all parts of your business. For this purpose, you will require Ethernet cabling, a router, and several switches, especially if you are setting up a larger network to cater to all your employees. You will also need a modem for connecting your network to the outside world. With that modem, you will also need an internet connection from a provider.

## Multi-function Printer

Information is organized, manipulated, and moved electronically in today's world. However, there are people who still love paper. If the information is electronic, it has to be printed. Whereas, if the information is printed, it needs to be scanned. If it has to be sent somewhere else, then it has to be faxed.

Buying one machine that can do all three services will help you save time as well as money.

## Smartphone

Time is money, and communicating effectively and timely, will help you earn money or save you money. Having access to your office email with the help of your smartphone can offer a lot of benefits and convenience for you.

## Shredder

Just as quickly information is transferred to paper, in the same way, it has to be destroyed too. Your business is responsible for the information that it possesses. It can be the personal information of an employee, clients' list, a client's sensitive material or a confidential memo. Either way, you are responsible for the information, and you need to make sure that it does not land in the wrong hands as this can cost your company its reputation. Therefore, a shredder is necessary for every company.

## Mailing Equipment

Documents, product samples, catalogs, and statements are only a few examples of the items that have to be shipped out of your company. The proper mailing equipment like scales and postage software can save your company valuable time and money.[27]

---

27 The Balance (2019). *Essential Office Equipment for Starting a Business.* Retrieved from https://www.thebalancesmb.com/essential-office-equipment-for-starting-a-business-2533797

# Equipping Your Business on a Budget

Equipping your business requires determining your equipment needs, then acquiring the items that you need and finally using that equipment productively.

Manufacturers, retailers, and service providers have different equipment needs. There is not a single appropriate collection of equipment and other physical assets, which will make sure that you earn profits and succeed. Every business owner has to determine what types of equipment, tools, furnishings, vehicles, and other items will be needed to properly run the business.

To help you in making that assessment, you will have to determine the equipment needs. Doing so will help you to acquire the items that you need, after which you will have to train your employees to use the equipment productively in the business.

# Determining your Equipment Needs

The type of business that you conduct will largely dictate what you need in order to run it smoothly. Nothing is exactly as mentioned in the articles or books. It all depends on the business owner. Some points that you may want to consider are:

## Acquire only what you need

One main advice is that you should never acquire any equipment or other fixed assets that your business does not need. Fixed assets represent long-term investments of capital. In many cases, the recovery of the money you spend on assets will take up to several years. Therefore, unless you have other financial resources, it is best to avoid acquiring any asset that will not bring a significant increase in your profits, efficiency, or productivity.

## Focus on function over form

When addressing the needs of the company, you will have to focus on functionality over form. For example, a previous job may have left you with the feeling that you need an ornate desk and a set of limited edition lithographs to give your office an environment of professionalism. However, if you think about it, you can be just as effective with lesser expensive furnishings and artwork.

**Perform a cost-benefit analysis**

For any item that is inexpensive, you can easily decide on whether or not to buy it by assessing if the item is something that the business really needs, rather than purchasing it because you want it or you think you need it.

When buying a fixed asset, you need to put the habit of performing a thorough cost-benefit analysis to determine whether the expected acquisition and operational costs will be completely recovered through the expected increases in earnings or savings over the asset's life. This analysis needs to be conducted before proceeding with the acquisition because you will rarely make a profit when disposing off a non-productive asset.

**Common equipment needs**

Every business will have these basic needs in common; therefore, you will need to invest in:

- Communications equipment

- Computer equipment[28]

---

28    Wolters Kluwer (2019). *What to Consider When Equipping Your Business*. Retrieved from https://www.bizfilings.com/toolkit/research-topics/office-hr/what-to-consider-when-equipping-your-business

If you are starting out and have just a few employees, then, in that case, you will need very minimal equipment. The basics include desks, chairs, computers, and peripherals, including monitors and printers. Research and careful shopping can help in equipping your office on a budget.

## Computers

Computers are key pieces of equipment. One of the biggest decisions is whether to choose a desktop, laptop or a combination of the two. Business users that need to go out on the road need to consider laptops. When shopping for computers, you need to look for machines that will last long before having to upgrade them. Look for small business-class laptops and desktops from major manufacturers. These include more rugged components and the option for longer warranty periods as compared to most consumer computers.

## Peripherals

Peripherals include technological items such as monitors, keyboards, mouse, copiers, and printers. Flat-panel displays are usually the standard choice. You need to consider investing in larger screens or dual monitors for jobs that require extensive work with databases, multimedia or multitasking with multiple programs. All-in-one laser printers are a good choice for a small office. These can easily handle copying and scanning, along with printing in a compact and low-cost package. For offices that have multiple computers and employees, it is best to invest in a network printer that can accommodate the size of the business.

**Furniture**

The appropriate office furniture plays a vital role in the way your employees feel and the image that your business projects to clients that visit your office. You need to look for ergonomic chairs and desks for jobs that require a good amount of desk time.

This helps in making the employees comfortable as well as it reduces the strain on the body from working long hours on the computer. Furniture can also help in setting the overall feel of an office, whether it is an open working environment or a cubicle setup. You need to consider the image that you want to portray to clients who visit your office and then select furniture that fits it.

## Networking

Networking equipment is what connects a small office to the internet and to other computers in the office. The most popular choice for small and home-based offices is wireless networking. For home offices, this lets you share a single internet connection with your family.

A small office can easily put up multiple desktop and laptop computers to a single DSL or cable connection. You need to shop for the latest Wi-Fi standard that features greater range and bandwidth than the standards that came earlier.

## Shopping

Small office owners are usually on tight budgets. Therefore, you need to take a smart approach to shop for equipment. You will have to compare prices across different manufacturers and retailers. Use different price comparison search engines to find the best deals you can get online.

Do not forget to add in the shipping charges and compare the prices with the local retailers. This creates a difference, especially when ordering large items like chairs and desks. Also, check for discount codes, coupons, and rebates. Used equipment is also an option; especially when shopping for furniture.[29]

# How to Apply for a Small Business Loan?

For a small business to get off the ground and to keep operating, it needs to have financing in the form of a business loan. One form of small business financing is debt financing. Small businesses can apply to banks or other financial institutions such as credit unions for commercial loans. Usually, banks do not give loans to start-up companies, but they do give loans to ongoing businesses. The following are some major steps that need to be followed to apply for the loan.

### Reason and Amount of the Business Loan

It is obvious that a business owner will know the reason and the amount of the business loan that he requires. If the business is a start-up, this statement may not be applicable. Start-up owners may only be in the process of determining

---

29      Chron (2019). *Equipment Needed to Set Up a Small Office.* Retrieved from https://smallbusiness.chron.com/equipment-needed-set-up-small-office-3005.html

the number of funds they need and why. Business owners need to take some time to understand why they need a business loan and how much exactly do they need. Oftentimes, businesses are not able to address the question of how much they need until they actually prepare their financial statements.

## Visit your Local SCORE and SBDC Offices

If your business is a startup, you may want to get some advice and help from experienced executives. If you have access to a chapter of SCORE in your area, they are a good source of advice and help. SCORE is a non-profit, volunteer group of retired business executives. If you do not have one nearby, you can always get online advice and online counseling. You may also have a local chapter of the Small Business Development Center (SBDC), especially if there is a university in your locality. The SBDC is part of the Small Business Administration (SBA), and it serves to help existing and new small businesses. It helps business owners with the application process for a small business loan.

### Review your Credit History and Credit Score

If your business is a start-up or less than three-years-old, in that case, your personal credit history is going to be evaluated along with your business credit history. Before you apply for a small business loan, take some time out to get your personal credit history evaluated. Request for a credit history report from each of your credit reporting agencies and review them. If you see any errors, write a letter to the agency to describe the error and ask for it to be fixed. If there is an error that the agency is unable to fix, file a credit dispute report. Check your credit score too. A credit score of 700 is good, and it significantly increases your chances of being approved for a loan.

### Start Reviewing Your Borrowing Options

Look for the commercial banks available to you. You do not have to go only to the large, national commercial banks. You can have a better chance for a loan at the smaller regional commercial banks. Other non-bank institutions may also be options for you, such as the credit unions. Talk to the loan officer about your need for a small business loan. If they make such loans, pick up a loan application. There are many other options, such as the microfinance loans that give loans to startup companies. If one lender turns you down, another one may say yes. Therefore, you need to keep trying.

**Prepare your Business Plan**

This is the most important step. In order to get a small business loan from any lender, you will need a good business plan. Until and unless you have a good business plan, chances are that you will not even know how much money you need and how fast you can repay it. The business plan is in addition to the loan application that is required by the financial institution.

The business plan has many parts. A good business plan will consist of several years of past and project financial statements for your business. It will also include a statement of collateral or the type and value of assets you will use to secure the loan. You will also need to include an analysis of the market that your business will serve as well as a statement of your own experience.

## Plan a Presentation and Make an Appointment

For the loan office to give your application a second look, you have to make it compelling. Prepare a presentation of your business plan and application for your loan officer. Put together a professional package to hand to your loan officer along with a narrative and any financial statements, spreadsheets, charts, and necessary graphs. Be sure to include an Executive Summary since many loan officers will read the Executive Summary first and then decide whether they are interested or not.

Make an appointment with your loan officer and request enough time to be able to do a short presentation that consists of visual aids, based on your business plan. You need to be concise, succinct, and organized when giving your presentation. The interest of the loan officer in your application will all depend on your presentation. Therefore, you need to make it the best it can be.[30]

---

30      The Balance (2019). *How To Apply For a Small Business Loan.* Retrieved from https://www.thebalancesmb.com/how-to-apply-for-a-small-business-loan-393254

# Chapter 6
# What's Your Market?

The term *"niche"* is the most used in today's digital marketing world. The concept of niche is pretty simple. However, very few businesses understand it and implement it. As per the dictionary, the definition of niche is that it is a term that denotes or is related to products, services or interests that appeal to a small, specialized section of the population. One common path to success for small businesses is to find the niche market and establish a dominant position in that particular niche.

No retailer nor business is able to deal with all the things that people need. Therefore, segments are made for the population whose needs are not being met. This space is where a small business is able to penetrate into the market.[31]

When you are niche, you focus on being the best at what you do and for whom you are doing it. Everything else does not seem to matter. It simply means that you do not chase

---

31      The Balance (2019). *How to Find a Niche Market and Make It Your Own*. Retrieved from https://www.thebalancesmb.com/how-to-find-and-master-a-niche-market-2948380

trends, nor do you worry about the competition. You simply work to hone your skills and serve your market.[32]

# Why Is It Important to Have a Business Niche?

Every business in every field has to face competition. Whether you are an attorney, bookkeeper, non-profit consultant or a sustainability consultant, there are many other people who have the same profession as you do.

If a prospective client is planning on hiring someone else, you need to ask yourself why they should hire you for the job instead of any other professionals present in the field. One of the best ways to answer the question and demonstrate your value is to specialize yourself in a specific field. This specialization is known to be a niche. There are two benefits of doing so.

Firstly, you are able to provide more value to your clients because you have successfully honed your expertise in the area that is relevant to them and second, you limit the

---

32      Business2Community (2019). *The Importance of Finding Your Niche.* Retrieved from
https://www.business2community.com/brandviews/shelley-media-arts/the-importance-of-finding-your-niche-02109845

competition that you face.[33] When you have a niche business, customers look at you as a specialist in terms of knowledge, ideas, and products. That means your customers are more likely to make you their first port of call. Due to this perception of the customers, they are willing to pay a premium price for the products they receive because they perceive that the product will be of a higher quality as compared to what they would get from a broad-based company.

Higher prices mean greater profitability, which makes niche business a better lifestyle business, not only because the owner is able to earn more by doing less, but also because the owner is able to shape the business according to the personal interests, hobbies, and pastimes of the customers. This is what makes 'going to work' a much more rewarding experience. With a niche business, there is a great chance that you grow to become an even better expert in the area because you get more opportunity to learn more about a small market sector as compared to someone who operates a general business and has to spread himself in every area.

---

33      CC Marketing Online (2018). *Why It's Important to Define Your Business Niche.* Retrieved from https://www.ccmarketingonline.com/why-its-important-to-define-your-niche/

With your specialized knowledge of products and services, you have a marketing advantage. This makes attracting customers easier, and you do not have to go through all the marketing hassles to reach a scattered audience. With more focused marketing and communication channel, you know where you can channel your efforts in order to get the best results possible.

Niche business also helps with the 'online visibility' of your business. You are focused on a more concentrated range of products or services than the general businesses. This means that your information will be seen by search engines to be as 'authority website', therefore it will lead to a higher ranking. Lastly, once the word about your business is out, it can spread quickly to make you an overnight success.[34]

# How to determine if there is a market for your business idea?

So you have the idea for a product, and you believe that

---

[34]    Smallbusiness.co.uk (2019). *The Importance of Having a Niche as a Small Company*. Retrieved from https://smallbusiness.co.uk/the-importance-of-having-a-niche-as-a-small-company-2401322/

it is something that is going to capture the hearts and the minds of consumers everywhere. Or let's say you have a service that is not being offered by anyone else, but it is desperately needed. Before you jump into the business, you need to determine whether there is a market for your product or service. You also need to determine whether any fine-tuning is required. In simple words, you need to conduct market research.

Business owners usually ignore this step mostly because they do not want to hear any negative feedback. They tend to be convinced that their product or service is perfect, and they do not want to take risks tampering with it. Whereas, other business owners simply skip market research because they believe it is too expensive.

With all the other startup costs, it is not easy to spend money on research to only prove that you were right all along and your product would be a winner. Whatever the reason may be, not conducting proper market research can amount to a death sentence for your idea for a product or a service. Businesses do not pay attention to the background information mostly because they are in a rush to get their product to the market. However, only those companies are able to do good who do their homework properly. Before you start your own market research, it is best to meet with a consultant, a business professor or the local SBA district office. They can provide you with helpful guidance and guide you through with your first step in the market research. Market research should provide you with information about:

## Industry Information

When researching the industry, you need to look for the latest trends. Compare different statistics and growth within the industry. Search for those areas of the industry that are expanding and the areas that are declining. How can they be of your advantage? A thriving, stable industry is the key because you do not want to start a new business in a field that is declining.

## Consumer Close-Up

Your market research needs to start with a market survey. A thorough market survey will help you make a good sales forecast for the new business you would have established. To conduct a market survey, you need to determine the market limits or physical boundaries of the area where your business sells. Next, you will have to study the spending characteristics of the population residing in that particular location. You will also need to identify the purchasing power of the location depending on its per-capita income, its median income level, the unemployment rate, population, and other demographic factors.

You will have to determine the current sales volume in the area for the type of product or service that you are going to sell. Lastly, you need an estimate of how much of the total sales volume you can obtain.

## Competition Close-Up

Based on a combination of industry research and consumer research, you will get a clear picture of your competition. You shouldn't underestimate the number of competitors in the market. In fact, you should keep an eye out for future competitors as well as the current ones. You need to count the number of competitors, whether local or international. Study their strategies and operations, and you must have a clear picture of the potential threats, opportunities, weakness, and strengths of the competition in regards to your business.

When looking for an opportunity in the market for your business, you need to understand every aspect possible of what trends have been established in the industry and whether your idea would stand a chance in the market. You should make use of any sources such as the library, internet, and any other secondary research to know more about your competitors.[35]

## Ways to Find a Market for your Business

Now that you know that your idea will be successful as a business, you need to look for a market to sell your product or service to. Having solid information about what your customers want to buy instead of what you want to sell to them can make you save a lot of money and give you the peace of mind and sanity that you require. Here are ways to think about your business idea in a more critical manner before you are stuck with products and services that no one wants or needs:

---

35 Entrepreneur (2019). *How to Determine if There is a Market for your Business Idea.* Retrieved from https://www.entrepreneur.com/article/240164

## Define your Target Market

The secret is to point out exactly who your target customer is, but the hard part is figuring it out. The best way is to start by asking the 'who', 'when', 'how' and 'why' in regards to your target market. Think about the basic demographics like gender, age, location, family income, and education levels. You can include information such as hobbies, interests, and life goals. Next, try to understand when clients will be looking for you and how will they find your business. Lastly, determine why they need you, and why are you the solution for their needs.

## Gather Information to Create Customer Profiles and Segments

The more data you collect, you have a better chance in creating a customer persona that is a reflection of the behavior of the segment that you are targeting. Look for all the places where you are able to collect data. You can use means like customer surveys, phone interviews, exit surveys, and Google Analytics.

## Apply the Data to your Business

Once you have gathered the data and you are aware of who your client base is, it is now time to take action. Determine the different ways that may or may not work for your client base. Try reaching your audience and develop a relationship with them. Make use of different social media platforms to stay in touch with them.

## Evaluate and Test Your Decisions

Once you have selected your plan of action, make sure that it can actually work. After implementing your market research, try getting as much feedback as you can. You can also go back to testing to make sure that your marketing strategy is working. If you accidentally choose a target market that is not complying with your business, you can always change it. Some entrepreneurs fear that they will be locked in a decision that they have once taken. It takes a while to exactly identify your market but once you have successfully done so, be sure to savor the fruit of your hard work.[36]

---

36      DreamHost (2019). *7 Steps to Identify a Target Market for Your Online Business*. Retrieved from https://www.dreamhost.com/blog/identify-

# Find a Market Related to the Niche Business

When selecting a niche business, you do not want to take much time. However, you want to get running instead of just waiting around. By doing so, you can test your ideas and enter the market sooner and learn from the mistakes you make and try to succeed in the market. So, if in the first attempt, your business does not take off as expected, you can always take what you have learned from past experiences and move forward with new and better ideas.

With the help of these few steps, you can easily determine your market and find your niche.

### Identify your Interests and Opinions

One step, to begin with, is to make a list of 10 topical interests and passion areas. Business is not an easy step. If you are working in an area that you are not interested in, then you will eventually quit, especially when you are a first-time business owner.

---

target-market-for-business/

This does not mean that you need to find the perfect fit. If you are passionate about an aspect of the business, you need to stick to it. If you are not really that interested in the topic, you may not have the interest to stay in that business.

**Identify Problems you can Solve**

When you have a list in your hand, you are now ready to narrow down your options. To set up a profitable business, you need to find the problems that your customers face in their lives. Then you have to determine whether or not you have the capability to actually solve them. You can identify these problems by conducting a one-on-one conversation with them, create discussion forums or by researching keywords.

**Research your Competition**

Your competition is what will show you that you have found a niche that is profitable. However, for that, you need to conduct a thorough analysis of those competitions. Create a spreadsheet and start logging in all of the competing sites that you are able to find. Then determine whether there is still scope in that area and if you are going to stand out in the crowd. Some hints that show you that you can enter a niche market and be successful include sites with low-quality content, lack of transparency, and lack of paid competition.

**Determine the Profitability of your Niche**

By now, you must have a good idea of what niche market you are entering into. At this point, it is imperative to get an idea of how much money you will be able to make in your niche.

**Test Your Idea**

By now, you have all the information you require to choose a niche. The only thing left is to test your idea. One simple way is to set up a landing page for the pre-sales of a product that you are planning on developing. Then, you can drive the traffic to this page with properly paid advertisement.

# Potential Markets

Potential markets are the most important part of the growth of a business. A potential market is a group of consumers who are interested in the market offer. A business may seem satisfied with the sales and the performance today; however, it does not mean that it has enough potential market for the future. This problem can be solved by making a decision to solely focus on the potential market of the business. By paying attention to the potential market, not only does a business increase its market share, but it also ensures that the market share will increase for the future.

The first step is to identify the potential market with your current audience. For this purpose, one has to go outside of the current market and look for people that fall in a certain age group, sex orientation, and certain socioeconomic status, and study their needs. You can also expand within the groups of people that you are already selling to or you can always choose a new customer group that you have never thought of before.

The next step is to find a purpose. The potential market is something that you can look forward to in the future, and it is a market that will surely make your future money. However, you cannot run a business without a purpose. It is necessary that you set goals for the future. You can choose to depend on your current sales, but that will not benefit you for the future. Understanding the potential market proves that you and your business have a future.

## Types of Potential Market

There are so many types of potential markets. You can find one every time you think of a new customer that you are willing to sell to. To determine the potential market, you need to brainstorm with your team and consider every kind of person that may be interested in your product. You ought to focus on the largest groups, but you must still try hard to catch the smaller ones.

To find your potential market, you need to give a lot of time to look for the potential market for all the products you offer. This process goes on all year long. You will need a new market for every new year. You can come up with new products that will grab a new potential market, but you always need to be prepared for the next product that you are planning on developing. Searching for a potential market is a continuous process, so you do not miss anyone. Eventually, a time will come when you would have just tapped every target market that you have identified.

Once you have identified the potential market for your products, the key is to convey the right message to the right person at the right time. Now is the time when you need to think of ways of establishing a connection with them.

This process requires not only using the right message but also the right marketing channels and the proper communication media.

The next step includes identifying your marketing budget to make sure that it leaves a significant impact on your market. Tapping into new potential markets is not an easy task, and it requires thorough planning to do so.[37]

---

37      The Balance (2019). *Identifying Opportunity in New Potential Markets*. Retrieved from https://www.thebalancesmb.com/identifying-opportunity-in-new-potential-markets-4043634

# Chapter 7
# Marketing

Marketing is the process of getting the right goods or services to the right people at the right time at the right place with the right price by using the right promotional techniques and using the appropriate people to provide customer service that is associated with those goods or services.

This concept is called the *"right"* principle, and it is the basis of all marketing strategies. Simply put, marketing is the process of finding out the needs and wants of potential buyers and then providing the goods and services that meet or exceed the expectations of the buyers. Marketing is all about creating exchanges. An exchange takes place when two parties have something of value and give it to each other to satisfy their respective needs or wants.

In exchange, a consumer trades his money for a good or service. Sometimes, the exchange is non-monetary. For example, someone who volunteers for a company receives a T-shirt in exchange. People have a misconception that there is no difference between marketing and sales. However, they are two different things that are part of a company's strategy. Sales incorporate the process of selling the products and services of the company to its customers, whereas marketing is the process of communicating the value of a product or service to the customers, so the product or the service is sold.

Marketers use the *"right"* principle. For example, if a salesperson does not have the right product for a potential customer when he wants it at the right price, the potential customer will not exchange money for the product. The *"right"* principle tells us that marketers have control over many factors that determine marketing success.

## The Marketing Concept

Successful organizations have adopted the marketing concept. The marketing concept is based on the *"right"* principle. The marketing concept refers to the use of marketing data to focus on the needs and the wants of customers to develop marketing strategies that not only satisfy the needs of the customers but also accomplish the goals of the organization.

An organization uses the marketing concept when it identifies the needs of the buyer, then produces the goods, services or ideas that will satisfy those needs. The marketing concept is directed toward satisfying customers by offering value. Marketing concept involves:

- Focusing on the needs and the wants of the customers so that the organization can easily differ its products from its competitors. The products can be goods, services or even ideas.

- Including all the activities of the organizations such as production and promotion to fulfill the needs and wants of the customer.

- Achieving the long-term goals of the organization by satisfying customer wants and needs.

One important key to understanding the marketing concept is to know that the marketing concept means the product has been created after market research has been conducted. The product has been created to identify the needs and the wants of the customers. The products are not just created by the production department, and then the marketing department just comes up with ways to sell them.

No, that's not how it works. An organization that uses the marketing concept makes use of the data about potential customers to make the best product, service, idea, and marketing strategies to support it.[38]

# Importance of Marketing

How you market your business determines if the enterprise will be successful or not. Marketing is a tool that is used to create and maintain demand, relevance, reputation, competition and more. Without marketing, your business is likely to close down due to lack of sales. The following are 9 reasons why marketing is important and why every business needs it:

### Marketing is an Effective Way of Engaging Customers

It is important for businesses to engage with their customers. Marketing is a tool that helps to keep the conversation going. Engaging with customers does not mean pushing your offers to your customers. Engaging involves giving your customers the proper information about your

---

38      Opentextbc (2019). *Introduction to Business.* Retrieved from https://opentextbc.ca/businessopenstax/chapter/the-marketing-concept/

products and your business. It is all about creating fresh content. When engaging with customers, tell them what they don't know and make it interesting and worth their time. The best platform you could use is social media, where you can engage with your customers. Marketing gives your customers a sense of belonging.

## Marketing Helps Build and Maintain the Company's Reputation

The growth of your business is correlated to the reputation of your business. Therefore, it is fair to say that your reputation is what determines your brand equity. The reputation of your business is developed when it meets the expectations of its customers. This business is considered to be a responsible member of the community. The customers are then proud to be associated with your products.

Marketers use effective communication, branding, PR and CSR strategies to make sure that the reputation of the business is maintained.

### Marketing Helps Build a Relationship Between a Business and Its Customers

Businesses need to build a relationship of trust and understanding with their customers. The marketing research segments need to be based on demographics, psychographics, and consumer behavior.

Segmentation helps the business in meeting the needs of its customers. Therefore, it gains the customers' trust. The product team ensures that the business delivers what it has promised to provide. This is what makes the customers loyal to the brand.

Loyal customers then have the confidence to buy more products from your company. The trust and the understanding between the business and its customers make your commercial activities even more rewarding.

### Marketing Is a Communication Channel Used to Inform Customers

Marketing helps in informing your customers about the products and services that you are offering them. Through marketing, the customers get to know more about the value of the products, their usage, and the additional information that may prove helpful to the customers. Marketing creates brand awareness and makes the business stand out. Due to the tough competition in the market, you need to inform your customers about the discounts to convince the customers.

**Marketing Helps to Boost Sales**

Marketing uses different ways to promote your products and services. Once the product has been advertised, it is on the radar, and it increases your chances of selling it. Customers will want to try your products and services, and ultimately, this would lead them to purchase your product.

When customers are happy about your products or services, they become your brand ambassadors without you even knowing about it. They will spread the word and eventually your sales will increase. Your job is to make sure that you offer high-quality products and services that compliment your marketing efforts.

**Marketing Aids in Providing Insights about your Business**

Every marketer understands the need for targeting the right audience. However, you need to have the right content to share with that audience. Your marketing strategies help you in establishing what business message will convince your target audience. When you are at this point, you need to test different messages and see what works the best. Once you have tested the different sets of messages on your target audience, you will find what works and what does not. It provides you with the insight that you need for you to avoid guessing.

## Marketing Helps Your Business to Maintain Relevance

Every marketer knows the need for disrupting the customer's opinion about other products. However, you should not take this for granted. Most businesses assume that their brand will always be the client's favorite because they have never complained. This is the wrong approach. You always need to find new ways to remain at the top of the customer's mind.

Every relationship needs maintenance. Marketing helps your business maintain a good relationship with customers. You should not focus on gaining new customers before retaining the present ones.

**Marketing Creates Revenue Options**

During a startup, your options may seem thin due to being tight on cash. However, as your marketing strategies generate more customers and revenue opportunities, you will start getting more options.

Having more options will give you the courage you need to enter new markets. You will have the freedom to let go of demanding customers and target new customers. Without marketing, you will be forced to continue working with clients who you have outgrown and pay only peanuts.

**Marketing Helps the Management Team to Make Informed Decisions**

Every business has problems like what, when, for whom, and how much to sell the product for. There is a very vigorous process to determine the answers to these questions. As a result, the business relies heavily on marketing mechanisms to make these decisions.

These mechanisms serve as a reliable link between your business and society. They cultivate the mind of the people, educate the public, and convince them to make the purchase.[39]

# Marketing Methods

According to its definition, marketing method is a long-term, forward-looking approach to planning with the fundamental goal of achieving a sustainable competitive advantage. Product, Price, Place, and Promotion are known as the 4Ps of marketing. The term 'marketing method' is a mix of these factors that you need to consider when marketing your product to a particular group of customers. That being said, let's look at a few of the most practiced marketing methods

# Digital Marketing

Digital marketing incorporates all the marketing efforts that use an electronic device or require the internet. Businesses influence digital channels like search engines, social media, email, and other websites to connect with their

---

39      Business2Community (2019). *Why is Marketing Important? 9 Reasons Why You Really Do Need It.* Retrieved from https://www.business2community.com/marketing/why-is-marketing-important-9-reasons-why-you-really-do-need-it-02186221

current and prospective customers. Digital marketing is defined by the use of different digital tactics and channels that are used to connect with customers online. From the website to a business' online branding assets, digital marketing is a huge umbrella in which digital advertising, email marketing, online brochures and a lot more falls in.[40]

## How Does Digital Marketing Work?

Digital marketing is no different than traditional marketing. Smart organizations develop beneficial relationships with prospects, leads, and customers. However, digital marketing has replaced almost all kinds of traditional marketing because it is designed in a way that can be used to reach today's consumer.

Most of digital purchasing begins online. With that being the case, having an online presence is necessary regardless of what you plan on selling. The key is to develop a digital marketing strategy that puts you in all the places where your followers are hanging out. Then with a variety of digital channels, you can connect with them in many ways. You will

---

40      Hubspot (2019). *What is Digital Marketing?* Retrieved from https://blog.hubspot.com/marketing/what-is-digital-marketing

also need content, social media presence, search engine optimization, advertising, and email marketing. When you add up all these pieces, you end up with an efficient, easy-to-operate digital marketing machine.

## Benefits of Digital Marketing

Having a strong digital presence will help in different ways:

- It becomes easier to create awareness and engagement before and after the sale

- It will help convert new buyers into returning customers who would buy more

- It will kick-start word of mouth and social sharing

- It shortens the buyer's journey by presenting the right offers at the right time.[41]

---

41    Digital Marketer (2019). *The Ultimate Guide to Digital Marketing.* Retrieved from https://www.digitalmarketer.com/digital-marketing/

## Disadvantages of Digital Marketing

Digital marketing has some limitations too. The limitations are:

- Dependability on technology

- Security, privacy issues

- Maintenance costs due to a constantly growing environment

- Higher transparency of pricing and increased price competition

- Worldwide competition through globalization[42]

## Guerilla Marketing

The word *"guerilla"* seems very intense. It raises sights of rebellion and conflict. If it is put next to *"marketing,"* it gets even more confusing. Guerilla marketing is not some kind of combative form of communication. It is an unconventional form of inbound marketing. It raises brand awareness among a lot of audiences without interrupting

---

42 Sinan Soft (2019). *Advantages and Disadvantages of Digital Marketing.* Retrieved from https://sinansoft.com/blog/advantages-and-disadvantages-of-digital-marketing/

them. Due to its unconventionality, it is not easy to explain. Guerilla marketing is best understood when it is observed. Guerilla marketing is somewhat associated with guerilla warfare. In the warfare context, guerilla tactics depend on the element of surprise. In marketing, guerilla techniques mostly play on the element of surprise. It is set out to create highly unconventional campaigns that will catch people unexpectedly in their daily routines.

# Types of Guerilla Marketing

There are a few sub-categories of guerilla marketing. These are:

### Outdoor Guerilla Marketing

This adds something to the already existing urban environments such as putting something removable onto a statue or putting up temporary artwork on the street.

### Indoor Guerilla Marketing

Just like outdoor guerilla marketing, it is almost the same. The only difference is that it takes place in indoor locations such as train stations, shops, and university campus buildings.

### Event Ambush Guerilla Marketing

Using the audience of an event such as a concert or a sporting game to promote a product or a service in a way that is noticeable without consent from the event management.

### Experiential Guerilla Marketing

This includes all of the above-mentioned guerilla marketing, but it is executed in a way that requires the public to interact with the brand.[43]

### Advantages of Guerilla Marketing

- **Low cost** – The executions may be simple yet effective depending on the type of Guerilla Marketing Strategy used. You can use your product to do the execution like using stencil drawings on the sidewalks.

---

43      Hubspot (2019). *What is Guerilla Marketing? 7 Examples to Inspire Your Brand.* Retrieved from https://blog.hubspot.com/marketing/guerilla-marketing-examples

- **Unconventional** – Guerilla marketing requires your imagination. It offers the indirect, subtle, and creative attempt to sell products or services. Many customers appreciate this trait of Guerilla Marketing.

- **Potential for Virality** – It has one of the highest potentials to go viral among many other marketing strategies. Therefore, it is so attractive. It can go viral by word of mouth, posts on social media or even just ads on traditional media. Guerilla marketing has the ability to gain free publicity from your customers by their own free will.

- **Complementary** – Guerilla marketing has the ability to bear attention or complement the existing marketing initiatives and activities by the company. It can also be used to promote social media engagement.

**Disadvantages of Guerilla Marketing**
- **Time Consuming** – Guerilla marketing may be low in cost and potentially edgy; however, it can take a lot of time to conceptualize, organize, and execute.

Its success impacts largely on how much time you have invested in thinking through the strategy carefully.

- **Measurability** – It is difficult to measure the results of the campaign because it is not easy to trace the reach and the results of the campaign. Consumers would interact randomly with the prop or the campaign. During the interaction, the experience is shared on social media platforms among unknown amount of people at an unknown rate.

- **Unpredictability** – It is almost impossible to guarantee the number of impressions it will gain on social media. It does not even guarantee that any of your consumers will even notice it.

- **Misinterpretation** – No two people will get the same interpretation of the message that is being communicated due to the mysterious nature of the Guerilla Marketing Campaign. The mysterious nature of the campaign makes it shareable; however, it can also work to its disadvantage.

- **Environmental Factors** – Guerilla Marketing executions are dependent on environmental factors like weather, poor timing, political unrest, issues with the venue, etc. This may end the execution, cause delays or sometimes cancellations with the change in interpretations of the intended message.[44]

# Relationship Marketing

Relationship marketing is an aspect of Customer Relationship Management (CRM). It focuses completely on customer loyalty and long-term customer engagement instead of just the short-term goals such as customer acquisition and individual sales.

The goal of relationship marketing is to create strong, emotional, customer connections to a brand that can lead a business, provide free word-of-mouth promotion, and gain information from customers that may generate leads. Relationship marketing is the contrast of more traditional transactional marketing, which focuses on how to increase

---

44 Think Premium (2017). *What Do the Pros and Cons of Guerilla Marketing Mean for Your Business.* Retrieved from
https://thinkpremiumja.wordpress.com/2017/05/15/what-do-the-pros-and-cons-of-guerrilla-marketing-mean-for-your-business/

the number of individual sales. A customer may purchase a product from one brand for one time only, but without a strong relationship marketing strategy, the customer may not come back to the same brand in the future. While organizations combine elements of relationship marketing and transactional marketing together, customer relationship marketing plays a vital role for many companies.[45]

# Advantages of Relationship Marketing

- Help deliver a more satisfying customer experience. Returning customers spend more than new customers. They provide you with the valuable data that you need to make important decisions about your products and services.

- Encourage dissatisfied customers to reach out to your company so you can find remedies to problems immediately. Encourage customers to spread the word about your business. Therefore, they become

---

45 Tech Target (2019). *Relationship Marketing.* Retrieved from https://searchcustomerexperience.techtarget.com/definition/relationship-marketing

goodwill ambassadors of your company on your behalf.

- Stimulating future marketing campaigns from the start. Once you have a strong foundation laid, all that is left to do is replicate the template for your success.

# Disadvantages of Relationship Marketing

- It requires a commitment and business culture to support it. This includes customer service representatives to the top management.

- It can be expensive because it takes time to properly cultivate customer relationships. It can also be time-consuming in execution and in conclusion. In other words, it takes time to see results from relationship marketing which adds to its expense.

- Customers are eager to spread negative information as soon as they get to hear it. Social media, in particular, makes it much easier for them to do so. After that, it takes time for them to address the effects and reverse them.

- It can cause new customers to be overlooked or even ignored.[46]

# Word of Mouth

Word-of-mouth marketing is different from the natural word-of-mouth references to a company's products and services, as well as the results differ. For example, when a consumer has a wonderful time at a restaurant, he later tells about it to other people. Or if someone has had a great experience when using a product, he tells everyone what they know about it. Word-of-mouth marketing does not stop at the first interaction; it leads to a flow of follow-on interactions.[47]

Any organization that encourages people to spread information about a product, a cause or even the organization itself uses word-of-mouth marketing. Word-of-mouth is useful for-profit as well as non-profit causes such as political campaigns.

---

46 Chron (2019). *Advantages & Disadvantages of Customer Relationship Marketing*. Retrieved from https://smallbusiness.chron.com/advantages-disadvantages-customer-relationship-marketing-45503.html
47 Investopedia (2019). *Word-of-Mouth Marketing (WOM)*. Retrieved from https://www.investopedia.com/terms/w/word-of-mouth-marketing.asp

A company that manages apartments can encourage its tenants to refer their friends and family to that company if they are looking for a place to live. The company can give incentives to these referred customers by offering them a cash bonus or some other benefit.

Word-of-mouth is a popular technique that is used by medical professionals to share their patients with different specialists. A doctor can suggest a particular dental practice for patients. In the same way, the dental practice can refer patients to other specialists like orthodontists and oral surgeons.[48]

# Advantages of Word-of-Mouth

## Cost

Word of mouth marketing costs nothing in the business. If a customer is satisfied with a product or a service, he will tell his friends about it without any extra incentive, such as a customer referral program. Word of mouth can provide you with additional sales even if the company is not spending

---

48      Marketing-Schools.org (2019). *Word of Mouth Marketing.* Retrieved from https://www.marketing-schools.org/types-of-marketing/word-of-mouth-marketing.html

money on advertising. It is useful for small and local businesses that have a limited budget for advertising.

### Trust

Word of mouth helps in getting new customers to try new products and services. People trust their friends and family members, more than they can trust businesses. Traditional advertisements work under the principle of reaching as many customers as possible, hoping that someone will be interested in trying the advertised products. A single satisfied customer will tell a few of their close friends. However, a strong recommendation from a friend is more than what an advertisement can do.

# Disadvantages of Word of Mouth Marketing

### Control

A drawback of word of mouth marketing is that the business has a little control over when and how it occurs. The lack of control makes it hard for a company to increase the word of mouth marketing. Customers are free to choose whether they tell their friends and family about their experiences. Also, word of mouth is not always positive. Customers with bad experiences can also spread negative comments about businesses that can discourage potential customers from trying the goods and services.

### Expectations

Word of mouth marketing can raise the expectations of the customers about the products that are difficult to meet. A positive recommendation from a friend will convince the customer to try the product; however, if the product does not add up to his expectations, then that customer would be disappointed. Customers who do not have prior knowledge of a company and have no expectations are more satisfied when they try new products as compared to those who have unrealistically high expectations.[49]

## Transactional Marketing

Transactional marketing focuses on sales transactions. As a small business owner, you want to increase sales and

---

[49]      Chron (2019). *Pros & Cons of Word of Mouth Marketing.* Retrieved from https://smallbusiness.chron.com/pros-cons-word-mouth-marketing-52484.html

focusing on transactional marketing can help in achieving that goal. The other type of marketing is relationship marketing which focuses on building a long-term relationship with customers in order to secure sales in the near future. An example of transactional marketing can help in understanding how to focus on closing a sale instead of building a relationship.

## Product

For transactional marketing, you need to create a product that meets the needs of the customers. This is the beginning of the transaction. For example, a house cleaning product cleans walls better than any other products. Your aim is to satisfy your customers' need to clean stubborn marks and stains better than the current product they're using.

## Pricing

In order to intrigue the customers in buying your product once they realize that it fits their needs, you need to offer a very attractive price. You have to maintain a profit margin that you can live with while attracting the customers at a tempting price. In the example above, if your cleaning product is cheaper than its competitor, you will have to also provide an added incentive for customers to give it a try and find out if the product lives up to the claims about it.

## Placement

Placing your product where the customers can find it easily is important in transactional marketing. If the customer has to look for it to buy it, you may as well just lose the sale. With the example above, you would want to place your product in hardware stores, grocery stores, and convenience stores. It would be better that your product is placed at the top of the shelf. This way, customers who like your product and the price can easily pick up your product.

## Promotion

Your promotion for transactional marketing forces the customers to make the purchase immediately. You can choose to promote your product in stores or use online coupons to convince the customers to act quickly. Focusing on closing the transaction can increase your sales. The cleaning product can be featured in a promotion that persuades the customers to buy your product and clean those spots of their house, which the other products haven't been able to clean.[50]

# Advantages of Transactional Marketing

## Cost

Cost is one of the advantages of transactional marketing. Transactional marketers are very much concerned about making the sale. Therefore the cost of transactional marketing is less as compared to other campaigns that end up spending a lot of money on building relationships with customers. For example, certain transactional marketing campaigns cost nothing more than a phone call or sending out flyers. Since it is a relatively inexpensive effort, marketers can easily make their marketing dollars last longer with transactional marketing campaigns.

## Time

Time is another advantage of transactional marketing. Like cost, marketers spend less time on transactional

---

50      Chron (2019). *What is an Example of Transactional Marketing?* Retrieved from https://smallbusiness.chron.com/example-transactional-marketing-25886.html

marketing as compared to other types of marketing campaigns because they are focused on one sale at a time. Relationship marketers spend most of their time communicating with the customers and building a relationship with them; however, transactional marketers are not concerned about that. They spend less time in acquiring a customer who gives them more time to reach out to more people. The more customers you are able to connect with, the more sales you can generate.

# Disadvantages of Transactional Marketing

### Relationships

One major disadvantage to transactional marketing is the "one and done" concept. Long-term customers are not the concern of Transactional Marketing. The marketers of transactional marketing are instructed to find people to make a purchase one time only and not foster a relationship with that customer for more purchases. Customer loyalty is never important when it comes to transactional marketing. This is a loss of potential future revenue for a company.

**Reputation**

Another disadvantage of transactional marketing is that you cannot build a good reputation for your company based on customer loyalty and reviews. When you build relationships with customers, they become marketing advocates for your company by telling their friends and family about your products and services. However, when you want them to only make a purchase, you eventually lose that ability to build your reputation with your customers. People do not recognize your brand if you do not build good relationships with them.[51]

# Cause Marketing

Cause marketing is a young concept that has recently grown. Cause marketing is an effort between a for-profit and a nonprofit organization to raise money for a cause. However, both the nonprofit and the for-profit organizations can enjoy the benefits which the collaboration brings. The company expects to sell more products while gaining public

---

51      eHow UK (2019). *What are the advantages & Disadvantages of Transactional Marketing?* Retrieved from
https://www.ehow.co.uk/info_8087208_advantages-disadvantages-transactional-marketing.html

awareness of its values and its willingness to support a good cause. The nonprofit organization benefits from it financially with the help of a high public profile's marketing efforts. A cause marketing program is not a low-key donation to a nonprofit. However, one can tell the public that this corporation is socially responsible and interested in the same cause as its customers. The marketing efforts may come from the corporation's public relations and marketing departments partnered with the nonprofit's marketing.

Cause-marketing activities like product sales, purchase plus, licensing of the nonprofit's logo and assets, co-branded events and programs, and social marketing programs differ from corporate philanthropy, which consists of direct gifts to a nonprofit. The donations come from the corporate's foundation, and they likely support a particular program that is run by the nonprofit and can be of short or long durations.

Corporate sponsorship is almost like cause marketing because the corporation gives the nonprofit money to hold an event, run an art exhibition or conduct some other limited activity. The funds are collected from the community relations budget of the corporation or the marketing budget. Usually, the company expects a certain amount of publicity through billboards, public announcements, and promotional materials.[52]

# Advantages of Cause Marketing

Doing something that your customers want is a great idea. As per the Cone Communications Social Impact Study conducted in 2013, more than ninety percent of consumers want to be associated with companies that support social or environmental issues, whereas eighty-eight percent of people want to hear about company's efforts, and ninety-one percent wants products, services, and retailers to support issues that worthy.

The middle-market companies are more dependent on their close relationships with customers as compared to larger companies. Connecting on an issue that people have an awareness about can strengthen those relationships even more. You can do that with a cause that forms the right fit with your company, and through that, you could have a hit campaign. Supporters of the cause marketing concept state

---

52      The Balance (2019). *What Every Nonprofit and Company Should Know About Cause Marketing.* Retrieved from
https://www.thebalancesmb.com/what-every-nonprofit-should-know-about-cause-marketing-2502005

that companies receive significant benefits out of the activity, such as improved company loyalty, enhanced employee loyalty, and better customer attraction and retention. Theoretically, your message and your brand can be amplified by the ones involved in the cause. People who are devoted to a particular cause are dedicated and persistent.

# Disadvantages of Cause Marketing

At the same time, a company can end up making the wrong decision when forming a partnership based on a cause. No matter what kind of campaign the firm is implementing, the business focuses on performance and results in the end. That can leave the efforts being useless.

In the same way, a company can take a huge hit when it looks like it is only writing a check to buy goodwill. For a large company, the issue can be lost in the shuffle and can be noticed by a small percentage of customers. For a middle-market company with a limited range of products and services, there are fewer chances of the problem to be overlooked.[53]

---

[53]     National Center for The Middle Market (2019). *The Pros and Cons*

# Undercover Marketing

Undercover marketing strategies involve introducing a product to the consumers in a way that does not seem like you are advertising the product. It is a strategy within the broader technique of stealth marketing where the agents pose as regular people and market the products to people who are unaware of the marketing strategy.

It is a common practice for companies to employ people in positions of power or respect in their undercover campaigns. For example, a Turi vodka campaign hired a high profile nightclub owner to feature the vodka at his private party. This created an association between the product and the popularity of the host. The vodka could have been marketed by hiring an actor to visit the bars, order the vodka, and recommend it to other consumers.

Furthermore, the internet has created a number of undercover marketing opportunities. It is common for companies to pay others to create a positive review of products in blogs, forums, and video-sharing websites and in

---

*of Cause Marketing.* Retrieved from
https://www.middlemarketcenter.org/expert-perspectives/the-pros-and-cons-of-cause-marketing

the comment section of different online retailers.[54]

# Advantages of Undercover Marketing

Undercover marketing has its own pros and cons. Some of the advantages are:

- One of the primary advantages is its low cost. This technique requires less money, which means that a part of the marketing funds is spent on the initial phase. Once the product has been well-marketed, then the company can spend less on other advertising strategies, which eventually saves funds.

- Another advantage is the product popularity. The product is famous before it is even launched. Therefore, it becomes well-known within a short period of time as compared to regular advertising. Also, the product is discussed in public forums and in peer-to-peer communication. Ultimately, the popularity of the product reaches the global audience.

---

54 Marketing-Schools.org (2019). *Undercover Marketing.* Retrieved from https://www.marketing-schools.org/types-of-marketing/undercover-marketing.html

- Launching a product is easier and beneficial. It is a lot easier to plan and to execute.

- Some of the companies use channel management for a target audience. With this technique, people except for the target audience also become aware of the product.

- Undercover marketing helps in developing the company's name and reputation.

- It generates local interest and spreads knowledge about the product. Also, there is a consistency in sales.

## Disadvantages of Undercover Marketing

Undercover marketing also has some disadvantages:

- Negative reviews have the power to destroy the image of a company.

- Using false news in advertisement leads to the customers losing trust in the company, and once the customers are lost, the company loses almost everything.

- Once the undercover marketing campaign starts, it becomes difficult to stop it even if the effects are negative. The damage must have been done already.

- If your marketing strategy is not planned out properly, the public will end up not paying attention to the product. The company will have to spend an additional amount on more marketing.

- Marketing is really tough in the market, and there is a chance that your competitors may destroy your campaign. If they are successful in doing so, your product will lose its value even before it is launched.

- Any kind of negative marketing spreads faster. If there is a human error in the process, it cannot be easily rectified. If the company is not able to meet the demands of the public, it may lose its face value.[55]

---

55    Marketing Wit (2019). *An Explanation of Stealth Marketing with Suitable Examples.* Retrieved from https://marketingwit.com/explanation-of-stealth-marketing-with-examples

# Determining the Best Marketing Method

Before investing your marketing money in media, you need to study your market and the media that influences them. If you are confused about which marketing method to use, you are not alone. Most small business owners face the same struggles on how to allocate their marketing money.

Before you choose to invest your money, you need to step back and ask the five basic strategic marketing questions. The answers to these five questions will help you select the marketing method that will help your business in generating higher profit. The five questions are:

## Who is my target market?

This question may sound simple; however, it is necessary that you clearly answer this question so you can choose the right media to target your customers. Do you sell a high-end product or service that is targeted to the people earning a six-figure income, or are you selling a low-priced product for college kids? To clearly understand who your best target market is, you need to start by analyzing your own database and conclude who and what type of person is purchasing from you.

## What media does my target market watch, listen or read?

Once you have figured out who your target market is, the next step for you is to do some research about what media they pay attention to. The best way to find out is to ask them. Ask them the different names of publications that they have subscribed to, the associations that they belong to, the radio stations they listen to, the television programs they watch or the type of mail they open and read. You will discover things that will surprise you when you ask these questions.

## Which media can extend my message to most of the people in my target market, per marketing dollar?

This is the most important question that you need to ask yourself as a business owner. To answer this question, you need to compare the relative marketing investment of one media to another. You need an objective tool to measure what you are getting in return for your marketing money. A commonly used media is the CPM calculation. This CPM calculation lets you break down your investment into cost per 1,000 exposures.

**What are my advertising objectives and how well does this media help in accomplishing them?**

With the help of the CPM calculation, you can answer which media can extend your message to most people. However, it still does not give you the answer to how effectively it will meet your advertising objectives. If you are looking to advertise to a few people, then you need to narrow down your choice of media to only the ones that let you pinpoint those few people. When you determine your advertising objectives and choose only those media options that can help you meet your objective, you can quickly and easily narrow down the best media choices for you.

**How will the media allow me to measure the return on my marketing dollars?**

After all the efforts, it is the "return on your marketing dollar" (ROMD) that matters the most. You should never choose a media or develop an advertisement that does not allow you to track and calculate your outcomes. The most common complaint of advertising from small business owners is their frustration with not being able to track their results. This happens when you develop an ad that is untraceable, and you use media that makes it hard to track the response rates. After you have answered the above-mentioned questions, the only way to know for sure what will work best is to test, test, and test. Testing lets you know accurately what works and what doesn't. You need to test small in order to minimize your potential losses.

To test the different advertisement media, you will need to plan and come up with traceable advertisements and then develop a system to tally the results generated from it. Once you have determined the type of media that you know would be profitable for your business, then it is time to increase your investment in that form of media and maximize the returns on it.[56]

---

56      Business Know-How (2019). *Marketing Methods – Determine Which One is Best.* Retrieved from https://www.businessknowhow.com/marketing/method.htm

# Chapter 8
# Networking

Business networking is about influencing your business and your personal connections to bring you a regular supply of new business. However, business networking is more than that. It involves relationship building which can be a deceptively complex process.

Business networking is much more than just showing up at networking functions, shaking hands, and collecting business cards. Networking for business growth has to be strategic and focused. Not everyone you meet can help you in moving your business forward. However, everything you do can be driven by the intention to grow your business. You have the complete control over whom you meet, where you meet them, and how you develop and leverage relationships for mutual benefit.

Networking your business means being proactive. The core of networking is doing something specific each week that is focused only on networking for business growth. When you understand exactly what business networking is, you will find opportunities that may never have been discovered, and you will be making an invaluable investment in the steady growth of your business.[57]

Business networking is the process of creating a mutually beneficial relationship with other business people and potential clients. The primary purpose of business networking is to tell others about your business and hopefully turn them into recurring clients.

## The Benefits of Business Networking

- **New Contacts and Referrals** – The most obvious benefit of networking is to meet potential clients and generate referrals which you can then follow up on to add to your client base. Networking can help in identifying opportunities for partnerships, joint ventures or new areas of expansion for your business.

- **Visibility** – You need to meet and communicate with potential clients and business partners on a regular basis to maintain business relationships. Attending

---

57      Entrepreneur (2019). *What is Business Networking, Anyway?* Retrieved from https://www.entrepreneur.com/article/196758

business lunches and other networking events raises your profile and keeps you in front and in the minds of the right people.

- **Staying Current** – In today's ever-changing business climate, it is important to keep up with the target market conditions as well as the overall trends in your industry. Knowing the market is key to developing a successful marketing plan. Attending seminars and networking with your peers and your business associates on a regular basis will help you stay up to date.

- **Problem Solving** – In addition to the potential of increasing your business, you can often find solutions to your own business problems or needs by networking. For example, if your business needs the services of a bookkeeper, accountant, or lawyer, you can find the ideal candidate through networking. If your business is in need of equity financing for a startup, you may be able to find an angel investor or venture capitalist through networking channels.

- **Sharing Knowledge and Experience** – Networking is ideal for expanding your knowledge by taking advantage of the viewpoints and prior experience of others. If you are thinking of getting into the import or export business, you can get some valuable advice from someone who has done similar business internationally. Taking advantage of the experiences of others before you invest time and money in a particular venture can be invaluable.

- **Confidence and Morale** – Most business people are optimistic and positive. Regularly associating with such people can be a great morale boost, especially in the difficult phases of a new business. If you are not naturally outgoing, meeting new people regularly can boost your confidence. Also, you can form new friendships on a personal basis with like-minded people.

The ultimate purpose of business networking is to increase business revenue. The thickening of the bottom line can be immediately apparent, as in developing a relationship with a new client or developing a skill over time, such as learning a new business skill.[58]

# Benefits of Business Networking

Networking is crucial to everyone's growth, as well as it is most crucial for an entrepreneur. Without any solid relationship, small businesses can easily be dissolved. Building a successful business from the ground takes a lot of time and energy. Therefore, it is vital to have a proper network of friends around you to support you in all stages of your business.

The benefits of networking extend past support and into volition. The benefits include building up a network of people around you who have a similar passion and are headed in the same direction, which leads to increasing your likelihood of success. The following are the benefits of networking for entrepreneurs:

---

58      The Balance (2019). *What is Business Networking & What are the Benefits?* Retrieved from https://www.thebalancesmb.com/what-is-business-networking-and-what-are-the-benefits-2947183

## Connections

As we all have heard, "It's not what you know, but who you know". Running a successful business requires finding people who can help you in different aspects, starting from legal to compliance to payroll. Having pre-established connections with such people will give you opportunities when you need them.

Networking can open the door to developing friendships with successful and influential people that you may never meet on an ordinary day. The benefit of connections is where the "network effect" kicks in. The people that you network with have their own networks. Eventually, you gain access to those networks too.

## Opportunities

On your own, you have the ability to generate opportunities. Whenever you are gathered with a group of new and seasoned business owners, you have countless opportunities available. No matter what business you are in, networking will give you the opportunity to embark on a joint venture, join a partnership, speak at a conference or write for a journal, sell or buy a business, etc. The opportunities are too much to count. However, opportunities can come with warnings sometimes. Warren Buffet says that the most successful people in the world are those who say no to everything. You need to ensure that you do not jump on every opportunity that comes to you. Instead, you should examine each one and decide whether the opportunity is worth it or not. Otherwise, you will undergo "opportunity fatigue" by chasing almost every opportunity and not getting anywhere.

**Referrals**

The potential for an increase in business is the biggest reason many business owners decide to join a networking group. Not only are referrals generated through your network, but they may also be pre-qualified. Also, the person who refers you may give a recommendation for you. The hard work has already been done; all you need to do is follow up with the referrals to make them your clients.

**Positive Influence**

The caliber of your network is what will decide your success. It is important for you to develop a strong network of people who raise you up as a business owner. Fortunately, the people who network are mostly positive by nature.

**Advice**

A network offers a team of like-minded business owners who are able to give you important advice related to your business and your personal life. However, you need to make sure that you take the right kind of advice. No one knows the details of the situation that you are going through as well as you do. Therefore, instead of taking "do" advice from people, take "think" advice from them. Simply put, take advice from people who help you understand how to think about a situation and not from someone who tells you what to do.

**Increased Confidence**

Networking is especially good for people who are not confident enough. It provides them with a catalyst for growth by forcing them to meet new people. The more you push yourself outside your comfort zone, the more comfortable you become inside.

Networking helps you in reaching out to other people. You build soft skills which change you into a business owner because the ability to grow your business is dependent on your ability to make connections with people.

## Satisfaction from Helping Others

Helping others is necessary for networking. In fact, if you do not use your network to give back to others, it will eventually be useless. Every business owner has his own problems that require a solution. For a few of them, you will be the person who is uniquely suited to solve it. When you see that opportunity, take it.

## Raising your Profile

Many benefits of networking are that you are known by the people around you. By regularly attending business and social events, people will begin to recognize your face and become familiar with your story. After that, you can build a reputation as someone who is knowledgeable in your field, reliable to work with and supportive of others by offering help to people who need it.

### Friendship

"Friendship" seems like an unprofessional addition to the list of benefits of networking. However, business owners need friends more than others. The people you network with are like-minded; your friendships will form naturally. You meet them regularly, and it is easy to maintain the friendship over the long-term.[59]

# How to Expand Business Network

A relationship-building activity in business is nothing like building personal relationships. However, business relationships do have some similarities that require good interpersonal skills and communication. When it is time to expand a business network, it takes a bit of planning and design to affect the seamless relationship-building activities. Some activities you can do to increase your network include:

---

59      Entrepreneurship Facts (2019). *Top 9 Benefits of Networking in Business.* Retrieved from https://entrepreneurshipfacts.com/top-9-benefits-of-networking-in-business/

## Help Others

One way to grow your network is to help others grow theirs. Except for good karma, you will also get access to the other person's network. A kind gesture will let you reach out to that person to connect to someone in his network.

## Use Rapportive

Rapportive is a Chrome/Firefox mail app that lets you see the social profiles of the people you are exchanging emails with. The idea is to not only know more about the person's background but also start following/adding him on social networks. The reason being, your email interactions may come to a halt after the specific activity ends.

However, you and the other person both can log in to your social profiles. The objective is to stay in touch with them in any means possible. There are many times when the person you are interacting with changes jobs. Along with their jobs, their email id and number change too. However, they do not change their social profiles.

## Attend Offline Events

It is one of the best ways to expand your network. Do not restrict yourself to attending only events related to your industry. You need to be open to attending casual events like tweetups, coffee club or book club events. Feel free to exchange cards in all these events.

## Follow up

After attending an event, drop an email to all the visiting cards that you have collected. Add in notes like, *"It was great connecting with you at the event, we didn't get a chance to speak in detail. What is your company into?"* This helps in breaking the ice and gives you the chance to talk about their work as well as yours. At the same time, while using Rapportive, add them to your social network, especially LinkedIn.

## Use LinkedIn

LinkedIn is one of the leading social networks that allows you to create your online resume and build your professional network. Using your email id database, you can add your initial connections. You can participate in group discussions and get different answers, which would not only increase your visibility but also flaunt your expertise. You can go and meet those connections offline and build a much deeper connection with them.

### Request for Connects

Do not shy away from asking your network to connect you to the relevant people who have the ability to offer you business. If they do, please be kind enough to thank them and return the favor in the future.

### Give Free Advice

You can give out free advice on your LinkedIn account or on different social media platform so people can read and benefit from them. The more people read it and like it, the more interested they will get to know you. That way, your circle of connection grows.

### Be Genuine and Humble

No one likes to stay in touch with someone who is arrogant in nature. Nor does anyone want to introduce you to someone from their network. You should have a healthy attitude for people to approach you easily.

### Take Breaks

Networking may become overwhelming every now and then. Taking breaks now and then, going underground and then resurfacing, helps a lot.

### Remember Names and Professions

It is not possible to remember all the names and professions. Therefore, you can add a short name along with their company name, which could help in triggering your brain to know who the person is. Rapportive also lets you write notes that you can attach to the person's email id. That way, you can easily recall where you met that specific person.

### Send Gifts

It is a good way for people to continue remembering you. It can be very cost-effective. You do not have to give out expensive gifts. All you have to do is select a reasonable gift, order it, and get it delivered.

Different networking skills can help in building your network that will prove to be healthy for the future. After all, "Network is net worth".[60]

---

60      Your Story (2019). *13 Ways Business Owners Can Increase Their Network.* Retrieved from https://yourstory.com/2012/07/13-ways-business-owners-can-increase-their-network

# Chapter 9
# Support System

## What is a Support System?

A support system is an informal network of people that you can rely on emotionally or practically. The usual suspects of a support system are family members, friends, coworkers, and neighbors. They could also be members of voluntary organizations, religious groups, teammates or online buddies.

Nobody can make it alone. Everyone needs others to help us survive and thrive. We are all a society of teachers, doctors, builders and everything else, and we cannot do it altogether.[61] A support system consists of people that know and care about you. They may be family or friends. These are the people that know you, your highs and lows, and they are there when you need them or when life brings you down. On the other hand, they are also there when you hit your highs, whether in your career or life in general. They offer

---

61      Virginia Counseling (2019). *The Importance of a Support System.* Retrieved from http://www.vacounseling.com/building-support-system/

good counseling when it becomes hard for you to process your achievements and success. They are the people who will give you honest feedback and reality checks.

# A Healthy Support System

Even the most independent people benefit from human interactions. Having a support system to encourage and guide you through emotionally tough times can be crucial to mental health. However, cultivating this support system does not happen on its own. Support systems can take up any possible form, and they can include family members, friends, physicians, therapists or counselors.

Support systems may also include strangers or acquaintances that you may meet through a church, a support group, and an online community or in any possible context that provides you with encouragement and accountability. Your support system is not limited to those who are close to you. You need to seek out support from those who are outside your circle as they can provide a different and helpful perspective on the challenges that you are facing.

# What Traits Define a Healthy Support System?

Not all support systems are necessarily the healthiest for those they support, therefore knowing the foundation of a good support system can be the ideal first step in knowing how you can improve your own support system.

Some traits that come with a healthy support system include accountability, fellowship, the sharing of common experiences, and a sense of purpose. Having a support system provides a level of accountability to help in achieving your goals or triumph over adversity.

Whether someone is trying to give up an addiction, lose weight, finish a degree or just move forward from a difficult phase of life, a healthy support system will not let you give up and will not encourage you to do unhealthy or self-harming behaviors. A support system that provides regular accountability checks can operate as a constant motivating section.

Counseling and therapy will always be a valuable component of a support system. Friends and family may be well-meaning, but they might not always have the emotional tools that you may need to help guide you.[62]

# The Drawbacks of Negative People in Your Support System

### Negative people can affect your attitude

Negative people will discourage you, and they will do anything to drag you down with them to the dark side. As Robert Tew said *"Don't let negative and toxic people rent space in your head. Raise the rent and kick them out."*

### Negative feedback from negative people affects your thinking

Negative people are energy-sucking vampires. The problem with negative people is that if you hang around with them a lot and listen to them long enough, they start having an impact on your thoughts, and soon enough you realize that you are thinking negatively instead of positively.

---

62      Avail (2019). *What is A Healthy Support System?* Retrieved from https://www.availnyc.org/healthy-support-system/

### They are an energy drain

Negative people tend to be energy drainers. There are some people who walk into a room, and the energy level goes up, and there are also other people who walk into the room, and the energy level goes down. These people tend to suck other's energy out.

### It damages your credibility

If you surround yourself with negative people, you may not realize it, but other people will begin to judge you by the people you surround yourself with. If you hang around negative people, your mind starts getting filled with negative thoughts.

### Negative people do not provide any encouragement

Negative people are not only negative, but they are also very discouraging. They are good at making the negative stuff sound like it makes sense. You need someone who will encourage you and support you in what you do, not the opposite. You need someone to lift you up and not knock you down.

### They are hard to get rid of

Many people meet negative people in their lives, and a lot of them say that they would feel bad getting rid of them. It is best to end the relationships with negative people because of the huge impact that it imposes on their lives.

### Life is too short

Life is too short, and you would not want to spend it being around negative, crabby, grumpy or grouchy people. They tend to make life miserable, and you need a life of happiness. You want a life with quality people. Therefore, it is best to limit your contact with negative people and increase contacts with positive people in order to bring you joy and happiness.

### Negative reinforcement versus positive reinforcement

Negative people will reinforce anything negative that you say and will give you all the reasons as to why you are right in your negativity and toxic thoughts. They will make you believe in your doubts. On the contrary, positive people will tell you that you can do it, and will give you positive reinforcement, which is what you need when you are surrounded by doubts.

**They love drama**

Negative people thrive on drama. Also, they want to involve you as a character in the drama. Like Tony Gaskins would say, *"negative people need drama like oxygen, stay positive, it will take their breath away."*

**You won't grow**

If you are associated with negative people, they will celebrate in stagnation and negative thinking as they do not want you to grow. They are the people who do not want to grow, and they will discourage you from growing as well. The only way to move forward is to associate yourself with people who are also moving forward in life and will help you move forward with yours. The positive person has his foot on the gas pedal, whereas the negative person has his on the brake.

In the end, it is up to you to decide what kind of people you want to be friends with and the kind of people you are willing to spend your time with.[63]

---

63    Lifehack (2019). *10 Reasons Why You Should Avoid Negative People.* Retrieved from https://www.lifehack.org/352233/10-reasons-why-you-should-avoid-negative-people

# Benefits of a Social System in your Personal Life

One advantage of belonging to a cohesive society in which people help each other is that the group is more better equipped than a set of individuals to deal with threats from the outside. People have realized that the strength is in numbers and they take comfort in the company of others, especially in times of need.

To appreciate the impact of social connection on the state of your body, all you need is to consider what happens when it is cut off. There are two components to physical pain, an unpleasant emotional feeling and a feeling of sensory distress, both of which are associated with a particular brain structure. This connection between physical and social pain reflects the tie between the social connection and the physiological processes of the body.

In one of the recent studies conducted on the health benefits of social relationships, researchers have provided evidence that social ties and increased contact with family and friends are associated with a lower risk of death in young women with breast cancer. Another study presented a similar result with respect to surviving heart surgery.

In another study, 4775 respondents completed a survey that asked them questions about social ties like marriage, contacts with the extended family and friends and group affiliation. Each of the answers was translated into a number on the social network index with a high value, which means that the person had many regular and close social contacts. On the other hand, a low number represented the relative social isolation.[64]

In conclusion, people with more supportive friends and families are generally happier and more successful in life as compared to those who do not have a healthy support system. We thrive in supportive environments, and we need other human beings to reaffirm our existence. The benefits of a support system are as follow:

- **Gives us a sense of belonging** – No one wants to be an outcast. We all want to get a sense of belonging. We thrive when we are accepted and being accepted into a group and spending time with people helps us in keeping our loneliness at bay.

---

64      Scientific American (2019). *The Importance of Being Social.* Retrieved from https://blogs.scientificamerican.com/streams-of-consciousness/the-importance-of-being-social/

- **Gives us a feeling of self-worth** – Being accepted and called a friend reinforces the conviction that you are a good person with value.

- **Gives us a feeling of security** – A supportive social network is a source of advice, guidance, and motivation. We all feel comfortable in knowing that if we ever need assistance, we have people who will come to our aid.[65]

- **Increased physical health** – People who engage in relationships tend to be more active. They improve their physical health through different social activities. Additionally, they are also motivated to maintain their physical health in order to keep up with their peers.

- **Boosted immune system** – Studies have proven that socially active people have an increased immune system, which allows them to fight colds, flu, and other ailments easily. They also tend to have better

---

65      The World Counts (2019). *The Benefits of Social Support for Happiness*. Retrieved from https://www.theworldcounts.com/life/potentials/social-connections-and-happiness

eating habits because social gatherings usually incorporate food and meals. Eating with others usually leads to choosing healthier foods.

- **A more positive outlook on life** – Staying connected with others makes us feel more connected to the world, and it increases our sense of belonging. People who engage in creating intentional connections with others help in improving mood and the overall outlook on life.

- **Improved mental sharpness** – By keeping the brain active and engaged, you can sharpen your minds and reduce your risk of cognitive deterioration. People who enjoy conversations and friendly debates with their peers help keep their minds more active and fresh.

- **Longer, happier lives** – By keeping an active social calendar, people can increase their lifespan and longevity. They benefit from having a support system of peers who understand what they are going through and what they really need. These commonalities allow for deeper and potentially more fulfilling connections.[66]

# Benefits of a Support System for an Entrepreneur

The business world is no different than personal life. It runs on social connectivity, expanding networks, and fostering connections. In an era where the newest iPhone acts as an event planner and chauffeur, we still prefer conducting face-to-face meetings.

Entrepreneurs are the lifeblood of a steadily growing economy. The world is in need of young entrepreneurs and their innovative ways of thinking. However, just as much as the world needs them, they too need a support system.

Becoming an entrepreneur is risky, which is why this path is often not flaunted and is even discouraged most of the time. However, that is a major mistake, and it is the attitude that needs to be changed on a cultural level. The world needs individuals who are highly creative thinkers and who can offer a bird's eye view of the larger business world. No great

---

66      The Oaks (2019). *Five Benefits of Social Interactions for Seniors.* Retrieved from https://oaksatdenville.org/blog/benefits-social-interactions/

entrepreneur in the past has succeeded without proper feedback and support. Successful entrepreneurs surround themselves with people with those who have the same mindset, those people who challenge them and push them and brainstorm along with them. Anyone who has achieved recognition has mainly reached that point by working with others and by opening themselves up to new ideas.

It takes a lot of drive, gumption, and intent to be involved in a dynamic support system. This is the part where outside mentors step in and act as guides to young entrepreneurs so they can mature into well-rounded business people. These mentors can be industry veterans, peers or even former clients.[67]

A mentor/coach can serve as a one-on-one therapist, whereas the entire organization can play the role of group therapy. Someone who works as a mentor is most likely to have sympathy for your situation. Also, you need to remember that learning never ends. Even the smartest, most prescient entrepreneur does not have all the answers to

---

67      Huffpost (2019). *Why All Entrepreneurs Need a Support System.* Retrieved from https://www.huffpost.com/entry/why-all-entrepreneurs-nee_b_12468772

everything. By listening to fellow entrepreneurs, you are most definitely to learn something new with every interaction.[68]

These fellow entrepreneurs become your inspiration, your friends, your partners, and your emotional support community. They may not be your close friends; however, they will listen because they are keen to know what you have to say. Your social support will help you in figuring out what went wrong and what went right so they can use this knowledge to their mutual benefit. The following are five benefits of having social support for entrepreneurs:

## Learn From Each Other's Mistakes

It is an important function of your society to be aware of what is going on in your business and understand the complete story of what is happening in the business. If you are paying attention, then you will be able to see actions that others are using. It is a great way to avoid some major pitfalls in the business world by giving identifying the direction to

---

68      Inc. (2019). *Entrepreneurs Need a Support System.* Retrieved from https://www.inc.com/replacemeplease1455988044.html

take, and the possibility of being able to use their adaptations in order to make your business successful.

## Exchanging Tips of the Trade

By having other experienced people be around you to give you the right tips and secrets can help you tremendously. You will be able to start off smoothly and keep going strong when the times are tough. These exchanges about the tips of the trade will help you in having greater depth in your connections with these people. In return, you can give tips to your connections and reciprocate the help that you have received.

## Passing on Knowledge

One of the biggest functions of a community of entrepreneurs is to pass on the knowledge that has been gathered from experienced professionals to the less experienced entrepreneurs. However, this is also a great place to find a mentor or become a mentor for someone else.

## Making Connections

Networking is a skill that is always needed in business and in personal life. Making these connections in your social circle is important. Through these connections, you will know each other well enough that you can give them a reference if they need one and they will do the same in return. This way, you can do favors for each other and help your entire community to grow their businesses and move ahead.

## Learning New Business Skills

Your social circle can offer services and skillsets that will help make your life as an entrepreneur easier.[69] Entrepreneurs face a lot of challenges, which is why they need people to grant them access to increase their capital, cultivate talents, measure impacts, and gain moral support to move forward. Entrepreneurs need people to help them build bridges, especially to succeed in their businesses. A healthy

---

69      Inc. (2019). *5 benefits of Community for Entrepreneurs.* Retrieved from https://www.inc.com/murray-newlands/5-benefits-of-community-for-entrepreneurs.html

social circle is what provides the entrepreneurs with what they need in order to operate their businesses smoothly.

# Chapter 10
# Ready, Set, Go

By now, you may be having sufficient knowledge and information about establishing a business. By following the above-mentioned guidelines, you can easily run your own business and even guide other ambitious entrepreneurs. Not everyone sees themselves as an entrepreneur; however, the urge to start their own business does not come to everyone either. There are many reasons that may attract one to start his own business, as mentioned in the previous chapters.

As previously elaborated, in order to become an entrepreneur, one has to make various changes. Change is never easy and taking that step is a powerful start. Working for yourself shows a whole new side of you. Once you have decided to run your own venture, it means that you have gathered together all your entrepreneurial spirit.

Running your business is the best decision you can ever make because:

- It is a way of life where you will get rid of the "what-ifs" in your life. Taking this decision will remove any uncertainties that you have in your head. You have nothing to lose; rather, you have a lot to gain.

- With each step of establishing your business, you get to learn a lot along the way. When you become your own boss, you have to tap into topics that never concerned you previously. It may include topics like marketing, accounting, operations, and finance.

- Also, you become up to date with all the new technology, news, tools, etc. related to your industry.

- You become independent because you are sometimes required to make decisions on the spot. There will be times where you have to make important decisions without consulting with your team members. On your path to becoming your own boss, you will become more decisive.

- Running your own business is very exciting because you are following your dreams and your passion one day at a time. Even if you are not making sales on some days, you will still be motivated to do better.

- At certain points in time, while running your business, you have to be brave enough to make decisions because no one else will make it for you. When you become an entrepreneur, you step out of your comfort zone and expand your horizon.

- You start making new contacts and expanding your social circle.

- As an entrepreneur, you will learn to stand by your words firmly. You will understand that things do not happen as you plan them, rather you have to make it happen by yourself.

- Being an entrepreneur means making entrepreneur friends. This way you will realize that you are not alone in this journey.

- By the time you have taken this step, you have gotten rid of all the doubts you once had about yourself.

Being an entrepreneur is not easy. There may be days where you may even wonder why you made this decision in the first place. In that case, you need to understand the benefits you are gaining by owning a business:

- You are in control
- You get to build something

- You get to help people

- You have the option to live a more flexible lifestyle

- You have the opportunity to change the world

- You may even make more money

Despite all the benefits of running your own business, some people are still not able to pursue that path. There are many reasons that may stop them from doing so, some of which are:

- People do not know where to look for the right resources or the capital they need. They are not sure of how to find investors and how to make them invest in your business.

- Some do not know about entrepreneurship.

- They fear the stress of entrepreneurship and are unsure regarding the right products that need to be in the market.

- These people have a passion for their job and cannot think of leaving it. They are comfortable where they work, and they do not have a reason to resign and pursue a business.

- They are afraid to take risks and fear failure.

# What is a Business Opportunity?

A business opportunity is the chance to fulfill a need, interest or want in the market by combining different resources. An entrepreneur needs to understand this in order to survive in the business world. How to attain these resources? You can identify the resources by:

- Thinking outside the box. As an entrepreneur, you need to find the opportunities and create an innovative solution to keep your business ahead of the game. To think outside the box, you have to know what is inside the box. This means that you have to know what has been implemented in the market before you and what is currently available.

- Once you are done conducting your research, you need to take advantage of the opportunity. You need to take the risk as innovation does not come from certain outcomes; it comes from taking risks and trying new things.

- Do things that other businesses are not doing. You need to take a leap and offer services that others are not providing.

- Do not be scared to aim high. You can ask for as much as you want. Do not think that you will not get it.

Failure is inevitable and unavoidable. It has to happen at some point in life. When running a business, people will try and talk you out of it. However, you need to make mistakes in order to learn from them.

Failures, mishaps, and mistakes play an important role in teaching you what to do and what not to do. If you are not failing, it means that you are not winning either. You are just playing it safe. You need to challenge yourself to achieve bigger goals, which will differentiate you from the rest.

You need to encourage yourself to make mistakes and accept all the lessons that you learn from them. That way, you end up in a place of higher learning.

# Legalities

As an entrepreneur starting new a new venture, forming a legal entity is important for your business. A legal entity helps in standing strong on the basis of law while being able to establish a lawful partnership. The partnership may be of any kind from a sole proprietorship to a corporation. All partnerships are legally bound to each other and are held accountable for activities conducted against the law.

Once your business plan is ready, you can focus on keeping your company safe. Being cautious and taking proper legal steps to secure your business will help you from falling into pitfalls that you may come across.

- Do not let your ideas get out into the world, especially if your competitors can benefit from them. To protect your intellectual property such as trademarks, patents and trade secrets, you need to get your employees, business partners, and consultants to sign a Confidential Information Agreement.

- If you want to protect an invention of yours, apply for Provisional Patent. This keeps others from copying your invention while you focus on establishing your business.

- Also, you can include a non-compete clause that prohibits an employee from competing against you.

- The next step is to decide what type of legal entity is best for your business. It could be either Sole Proprietorship, Partnership, Limited Liability Company or a Corporation.

- As a business owner, you need to keep yourself and your business safe. Small initiatives such as opening your own mail, using passwords and other security measures, not storing sensitive financial data online, make a huge difference.

Except for the above-mentioned precautions, there is other legal documentation required when running a business. These documentations include company bylaws for corporations, meeting minutes, operating agreements for LLCs, non-disclosure agreement, employment agreement, business plan, memorandum of understanding, online terms of use, online privacy policy, apostille and many more as the business grows.

One of the most basic and important elements of setting up a business is its positioning. The success of your business depends on how well you position it in the market. You need to position your business in a way that you are easily found. Positioning includes the location of your business, pricing of your products, and how do you promote your business, online and offline.

Location is the most important positioning for a business. Despite the fame of online business, it is still important to have a business address. The address of your business has to be within reach of your clients. You need to find a location that will promote your business rather than demote it. The importance of location is:

- It increases brand visibility which means that location itself increases the ability of the business to market itself. When marketing your business, location matters the most. It has an impact on the placements of your advertisements.

- You want to be where your customers are. You want to make it easy for them to have access to your business. The location of the business creates a perception in the mind of the buyer.

- When selecting your location, you also need to keep in mind your suppliers since the speed of delivery has a huge impact on productivity.

- If your business is located in a convenient location to attract the customers, then you can be certain that your business will grow, as well as you can expect an increase in sales along with brand visibility.

- The location of your business can also affect the competition that your business faces.

- The location affects the total cost of operations.

- The location determines the state and the local taxes that the owners have to pay and the rules that they need to follow. Income tax and sales tax are different in different locations.

Regardless of the nature of your business, you need to have a clear picture of your business before you start looking for locations. You need to know what you need to have, what you want to have, what you will not tolerate, and how much you can afford.

Many startup decisions can be corrected with time; however, the decision to change is not easy once a bad location has been chosen. The type of location that you choose depends on the type of business that you are in. You need to think about each type of location space before making a decision.

## Home Based Business

In the previous chapters, I have discussed home-based businesses and how it is the trendiest type of business that entrepreneurs start within their home. As the business grows, entrepreneurs move to a commercial location.

With a home-based business, you do not have to worry about negotiating the leases. On the other hand, you have very limited room to grow, which becomes a challenge for you to accommodate employees and meet your clients.

## Mobile

Whether your business caters to the general public or any other business, if your business is related to a product or a service that takes you to your customers, then your ideal office is a car, van or a truck.

# Commercial

Commercial space has more options compared to retail. Commercial buildings and business parks offer office space that is meant for businesses that do not require enough amount of pedestrian or vehicle traffic for sales.

# Industrial

If your business involves manufacturing, you will need a plant or a warehouse facility. You need to consider free-standing commercial building that meets your needs. This includes manufacturing facilities, warehouse space, flex space, etc.

# Gathering the Resources

Operating a business requires a lot of resources. The resources that a company needs can be broken down into five broad categories.

- Financial resources

- Human resources

- Education resources

- Emotional resources

- Physical resources

# Equipment for Starting a Business

Establishing a business does not only require an office space. You will also need furniture and office equipment for your office space. You will need equipment such as computers, software, printers, fax machines, PABX, and network equipment.

# Apply for a Small Business Loan

For a small business to take off the ground, you will need financing in the form of a business loan. Small businesses can apply to banks or other financial institutions for a loan. You will have to follow a proper procedure to apply for a loan and qualify to receive it. The procedure has been explained in the chapters above.

# Your Market

When starting your own business, you need to know the market you are willing to cater to. No business can deal with all the needs of the people, which is why segments are made for those people whose needs are not being met.

When you have a niche business, customers view you as a specialist in terms of knowledge, ideas, and products. Customers are willing to pay a premium price for the products because they perceive that it is of the best quality as compared to the local markets.

With a niche market, you have a greater chance of growth and become an expert in the area. The niche business also helps with the online presence of your business.

Before you begin your business, you need to find out whether the market has space for your product. Not conducting the proper market research can become a death sentence for the idea of your business. It is helpful if you meet with a consultant as they can guide you through your steps to market research.

# Potential Markets

This is the most important part of the growth of a business. A potential market refers to a group of consumers interested in the market offer. By paying attention to the potential market, a business can increase its market share and ensure that the market share will increase in the future.

After knowing your market, your next step is marketing. Marketing is the process of getting the right products to the right people at the right time. This is called the right principle. Marketers use this principle to sell their products.

Businesses use the marketing concept to satisfy the needs of the customers and accomplish the goals of the organization. An organization that uses the marketing concept makes use of the data about potential customers to make the best product, service, idea, and marketing strategies to support it.

Why is Marketing Important?

- It is an effective way of engaging customers

- It helps build and maintain the reputation of the company

- It helps in building a relationship between the business and its customers

- It is the communication channel used to communicate with customers

- It helps boost sales

- It aids in providing insights about your business

- It helps your business maintain relevance

- It creates revenue options

- It helps the management team in making informed decisions

## Marketing Methods

A marketing method is a long-term approach which is used for planning the fundamental goal of achieving a sustainable competitive advantage. The 4Ps of marketing include Product, Price, Place, and Promotion. The marketing method is a mix of these factors that you need to consider when marketing your product to your customers. Some of the most practiced marketing methods are:

- Digital marketing

- Guerilla marketing

- Relationship marketing

- Word of mouth

- Transactional marketing

- Cause marketing

- Undercover marketing

# Networking

Networking is all about influencing your business and your personal connections, so you get a regular supply of new business. Business networking involves relationship building. It is more than just shaking hands, attending functions, and collecting business cards. Business networking has to be strategic and focused.

Networking in your business means being proactive. When you understand exactly what business networking is, you will find the opportunities that you never thought were there. Business networking is a process of creating a mutually beneficial relationship with other business people and potential clients.

The benefits of networking for entrepreneurs are:

- Connections

- Opportunities

- Referrals

- Positive influence

- Advice

- Increased confidence

- Satisfaction from helping others

- Raising your profile

- Friendship

## Support System

A support system is a network of people that is informal. You can easily rely on these people emotionally and practically. These people are usually your family members, friends, coworkers, and neighbors. Even voluntary organizations, religious groups, teammates, and online buddies can be your support system. It all depends on the level of relationship you have with them.

These are the people that know you, your highs and your lows, and they are there when you need them. They are also there when you achieve milestones in your career or in your life.

Your support system does not only count the people who are close to you. Your support system may include people outside your circle. Those people provide you with a different and helpful perspective on the challenges that you are going through.

Negative people always have a negative impact on your life. Some of the impacts include:

- They can affect your attitude

- Their negative feedback affects your thinking

- They drain the energy out of you

- They damage your credibility

- They do not encourage you

- They are hard to get rid of

- They will reinforce negative things in you

- They enjoy drama

- You will not grow as long as they are around you

For an entrepreneur, the support system is beneficial on a whole different level. Becoming an entrepreneur is a risky step, which is often discouraged. Entrepreneurs need a support system that will influence them to keep going. They need people who will challenge them and push them to move forward.

Entrepreneurs can make entrepreneur friends who will become their inspiration, friends, partners, and emotional support. They can learn from each other's mistakes, exchange tips of the trade, pass on knowledge, make connections, and learn new business skills. Entrepreneurs need positive people who can help them and push them to achieve their goals. A healthy social circle is what will give entrepreneurs what they need to help run the business smoothly.

This is all that has been taught in the entire book that is more than sufficient for you to start your own business. As you follow the instructions and the dos and don'ts mentioned, it will be a lot easier for you to walk the path of entrepreneurship.

# Learn from Your Mistakes

People see success as positive and failure as negative. Edison's quote shows that failure is not a bad thing. Through failure, you can learn and grow from your past mistakes. In business, failure is a common practice. Nine out of ten small businesses are meant to fail in one way or another.

The facts may make you uneasy and fear your choice, but it is worth knowing. Failing once or more than once does not mean that you have hit the end of the road, it simply means that you have taken another turn and that you are one step closer to success. As you move forward in life and encounter failures, you will learn valuable life lessons from those mistakes.

How do you learn from your failures and become a successful and productive individual as well as an entrepreneur? Here's how:

## Stay Humble

When you are doing well in life, it feels like you are unstoppable. There are no words that can give you the feeling that you are on top of the world. In this stage, when failure hits you, it hurts. It may even hurt so bad that you believe that you will never succeed again.

Staying humble helps overcome the dramatic feelings of loss and failure. When you are high on the feelings of success, you should never forget that you are human too and so, you should treat everyone with the same humility and respect that you expect in return.

When you are humble, you are mentally prepared for failures before they even come your way. Also, it will ensure that you do not become too proud of yourself. Always know that people who are close to you will help lift you up when things are not going as planned.

**Learn Learn, and Learn**

It is almost impossible to find a success story that has no failures behind it. Everyone experiences failure at some point in their lives. The key to overcoming obstacles and becoming successful starts with learning from your failures and mistakes. You should not be afraid to be held accountable when you are responsible for a failure in your business. It is possible that something could have been done differently to prevent the collapse.

**Embrace Change**

One of the ways to learn from your failures is by embracing change. Some people are afraid of change. They get caught up in their ways and therefore, they get used to their everyday routine.

When you fail, you have to change things drastically. If things are not going your way, and you have to start over, you have to sit back and determine the changes that have to be made and embrace them.

When you embrace change after a failure, you are encouraging healthy mental growth. If you want to be a healthy entrepreneur, you have to be mentally healthy.

**Filter Your Ideas**

Not every idea that comes to mind is a good one. When you are succeeding, it is easy to act on every business idea that comes to mind. It could be about a new product, a new marketing campaign, or anything that could generate more traffic. In such a case, you need to slow down. The best thing you can do to filter through your ideas is to take notes. You can either carry around a small notepad or download an app to make things easier.

As ideas pop up in your head, you need to note them down. Give time to your thoughts before you act on them. There is a saying that for every good idea, there are a hundred bad ones. Bad ideas lead to failure on a small as well as on a large scale. Note down your thoughts and go through them at some point later. In most cases, you will discover that most of your ideas were not as good as you thought them to be.

You can never be successful without failing. As you pursue your entrepreneurial dreams, you are definitely going to fail. It is often said that failure never stops people; it is how people handle failure that stops them. When you encounter failure, you need to tackle it head-on and learn from your mistakes.[70]

## Basic Elements to Start a Business

The most important element of successful entrepreneurship is personal dedication. Establishing a small business is not for everyone. Many potential entrepreneurs

---

[70]     Business.com (2019). *How to Learn From Your Failures: 4 Valuable Lessons.* Retrieved from https://www.business.com/articles/learning-from-failure/

decide not to go through with their own business due to the risk of failure or because they are just not that enthusiastic about their idea. When considering entrepreneurship, you need to ensure that you are passionate about your idea and that you are committed to making your business successful. You need to know that you are never really able to be your own boss. Even when you are the owner of a business, you need to answer to your employees, your customers, and the community.

If you decide to make the commitment to entrepreneurship, you will be ready to take the first steps towards starting your business. Once you have decided that owning a small business is for you, you need to make sure that the idea is compatible with entrepreneurship as well.

You need to carefully analyze your business idea and ensure that there is a market for the goods and services your business will provide. One of the best ways to support your idea for a business is to conduct market research and compile all the information you can get about the people who are willing to buy your goods and services. You should know what needs your business fills in the marketplace.

In the same way, you need to make sure that you completely understand the internal components of your business idea. You need to know and understand how your goods and services will be produced, as well as you need to acknowledge that anything can hinder your ability to offer your core products.

Be sure to keep in mind the cost, technical, and legal factors of producing your products and know what your business needs to address the different issues. Once you have completely analyzed your idea and have developed a strong argument of why it is feasible, you will have the resources and the tools you need to begin seeking the necessary finance for your venture.[71]

## Devotion to Achieving Your Goals

To achieve your goals, there are many different resources. However, there is only one thing that you cannot succeed without; devotion. By devotion, I mean staying focused and working consistently. Devotion means that you have to say

---

71 Wesst (2019). *Starting a Business Requires Personal Dedication.* Retrieved from https://www.wesst.org/2014/01/starting-a-business-requires-personal-dedication/

no to distractions, be patient, believe in the process, change your approach and strategies, and try new things while keeping the initial vision in mind.

To be willing to devote your time, energy and focus, you need to understand why devotion matters so much:

**It is the price you pay for what you are going to get**

Success doesn't come by itself, which is why not everyone is successful. When you are working hard to achieve your success, you understand its value. You begin to respect the work itself and build some qualities along the way.

**Devotion helps you build discipline**

At the beginning of your journey, you are not ready to handle all the success and the responsibilities that come with it. However, earning it with sweat and sacrifices gives you the discipline to deal with it.

**It teaches you to value**

Devotion teaches you to persevere, find ways to appreciate all you have and still aim higher, be patient, take action instead of waiting for things to happen, not blame others and take responsibility for anything you have or don't have in life.

Devotion gives you a purpose, and it helps you overcome laziness, procrastination, your doubts, fear of failure, insecurities, and bad habits.

## You make your own luck with it

Most people spend their lives waiting for things to happen. People with goals constantly do something and try new things to move forward. Devotion creates opportunities. Grabbing opportunities and making the most of them is part of devotion.

## It gives you results

The best measure of anything is progress. There is nothing that brings more results than devotion. Working on your goal itself is enough motivation for you to keep moving forward and saying no to distractions.[72]

---

72 Motivation Grid 2019. *The Reason Why Hard Work Is The Key to Success.*
https://motivationgrid.com/hard-work-is-the-key-to-success/

What is the difference between a dream and a passion? A dream is often a snapshot moment of idyllic perfection, whereas passion is an ongoing fire that compels you. If you plan on running a business, it will take passion to make it actually successful.

In order to run a business, you need to understand your passions. What makes you passionate about business? Think about the day in and day out operations that will keep you busy and excited. What is it that will get you in early, make you stay late, and go home tired but with a smile on your face?

Take time to discover your passion, and if you have a passion for the owning and sacrificing part of being an entrepreneur, then business is the path for you to take.

*"Pleasure in the job puts perfection in the work."*

*-Aristotle*

# Bibliography

Huffpost (2019). *10 Reasons Why You Should Start Your Own Business.* Retrieved from https://www.huffpost.com/entry/10-reasons-why-you-should-start-your-own-business_b_8046036

The Balance (2019). *The Benefits of Owning Your Own Business.* Retrieved from https://www.thebalancesmb.com/the-advantages-of-owning-your-own-business-2948555

PowerHomeBiz.com (2019). *12 Common Reasons Why People Don't Start Their Own Businesses.* Retrieved from https://www.powerhomebiz.com/starting-a-business/entrepreneurship/12-common-reasons-people-dont-start-businesses.htm

Due Inc. (2019). *4 Fears Holding You Back From Starting A Business.* Retrieved from https://due.com/blog/4-fears-holding-back-starting-business/

Grasshopper (2019). *6 Reasons Why People Are Afraid to Start a Business.* retrieved from https://grasshopper.com/blog/6-reasons-why-people-are-afraid-to-start-a-business/

Entrepreneur (2019). *How to Conquer Your Fear of Starting a Business.* retrieved from https://www.entrepreneur.com/article/302154

PowWowNow (2019). *How to Spot (and act on) New Business Opportunities.* Retrieved from https://www.powwownow.co.uk/smarter-working/spot-act-business-opportunities

Entrepreneur (2019). *Why Embracing Failure is Good for Business.* Retrieved from https://www.entrepreneur.com/article/315384

Ladders (2019). *Why Making Mistakes is Actually Good for Business.* Retrieved from https://www.theladders.com/career-advice/why-making-mistakes-is-actually-good-for-business

Law Trades (2019). *When Is It Necessary to Create a Legal Entity for a Startup?* Retrieved from https://www.lawtrades.com/answers/necessary-create-legal-entity-startup/

Young Upstarts (2019). *How Important is the Legal Department for a Startup Company?* Retrieved from http://www.youngupstarts.com/2018/06/28/how-important-is-the-legal-department-for-a-startup-company/

Upcounsel (2019). *Legal Entity: Everything You Need to Know.* Retrieved from https://www.upcounsel.com/legal-entity

Rocket Lawyer (2019). *A Legal Guide for Startups.* Retrieved from https://www.rocketlawyer.com/article/a-legal-guide-for-startups.rl

Investopedia (2019). *Sole Proprietorship.* Retrieved from https://www.investopedia.com/terms/s/soleproprietorship.asp

Investopedia (2019). *Partnership.* Retrieved from https://www.investopedia.com/terms/p/partnership.asp

Investopedia (2019). *Limited Liability Company (LLC).* Retrieved from https://www.investopedia.com/terms/l/llc.asp

Investopedia (2019). *Corporation.* Retrieved from https://www.investopedia.com/terms/c/corporation.

asp

Entrepreneur (2019). *The 10 Key Legal Documents for Your Business.* Retrieved from https://www.entrepreneur.com/article/236967

Alltopstartups (2018). *The Importance of Location in Business.* Retrieved from https://alltopstartups.com/2018/03/15/the-importance-of-location-in-business/

Azcentral.com (2019). *Why is Business Location Important?* Retrieved from https://yourbusiness.azcentral.com/business-location-important-3566.html

The Balance (2019). *The Different Types of Retail Locations.* Retrieved from https://www.thebalancesmb.com/types-of-retail-locations-2890244

Rosetti Properties (2019). *Retail Space Vs. Commercial Space – What's The Difference?* Retrieved from https://www.rosettiproperties.com/rosetti-properties-news/retail-space-vs-commercial-space-what-s-the-difference

Entrepreneur (2019). *Choosing a Location for Your Business.* Retrieved from https://www.entrepreneur.com/article/21830

Tenant Base (2019). *8 Types of Industrial & Warehouse Office Space.* Retrieved from https://blog.tenantbase.com/8-types-of-industrial-warehouse-office-space

Entrepreneur & Investor (2019). *The Importance of Location in Business.* Retrieved from http://entrepreneurandinvestor.com/the-importance-of-location-in-business/

Chron (2019). *5 Resources You Need to Succeed to Start a Business.* Retrieved from https://smallbusiness.chron.com/5-resources-need-succeed-start-business-23.html

The Balance (2019). *Essential Office Equipment for Starting a Business.* Retrieved from https://www.thebalancesmb.com/essential-office-equipment-for-starting-a-business-2533797

Wolters Kluwer (2019). *What to Consider When Equipping Your Business.* Retrieved from https://www.bizfilings.com/toolkit/research-topics/office-hr/what-to-consider-when-equipping-your-business

Chron (2019). *Equipment Needed to Set Up a Small Office.* Retrieved from https://smallbusiness.chron.com/equipment-needed-set-up-small-office-3005.html

The Balance (2019). *How To Apply For a Small Business Loan.* Retrieved from https://www.thebalancesmb.com/how-to-apply-for-a-small-business-loan-393254

The Balance (2019). *How to Find a Niche Market and Make It Your Own.* Retrieved from https://www.thebalancesmb.com/how-to-find-and-master-a-niche-market-2948380

Business2Community (2019). *The Importance of Finding Your Niche.* Retrieved from https://www.business2community.com/brandviews/shelley-media-arts/the-importance-of-finding-your-niche-02109845

CC Marketing Online (2018). *Why It's Important to Define*

*Your Business Niche.* Retrieved from https://www.ccmarketingonline.com/why-its-important-to-define-your-niche/

Smallbusiness.co.uk (2019). *The Importance of Having a Niche as a Small Company.* Retrieved from https://smallbusiness.co.uk/the-importance-of-having-a-niche-as-a-small-company-2401322/

Entrepreneur (2019). *How to Determine if There is a Market for your Business Idea.* Retrieved from https://www.entrepreneur.com/article/240164

DreamHost (2019). *7 Steps to Identify a Target Market for Your Online Business.* Retrieved from https://www.dreamhost.com/blog/identify-target-market-for-business/

The Balance (2019). *Identifying Opportunity in New Potential Markets.* Retrieved from https://www.thebalancesmb.com/identifying-opportunity-in-new-potential-markets-4043634

Opentextbc (2019). *Introduction to Business.* Retrieved from https://opentextbc.ca/businessopenstax/chapter/the-marketing-concept/

Business2Community (2019). *Why is Marketing Important? 9 Reasons Why You Really Do Need It.* Retrieved from https://www.business2community.com/marketing/why-is-marketing-important-9-reasons-why-you-really-do-need-it-02186221

Hubspot (2019). *What is Digital Marketing?* Retrieved from https://blog.hubspot.com/marketing/what-is-digital-marketing

Digital Marketer (2019). *The Ultimate Guide to Digital Marketing.* Retrieved from https://www.digitalmarketer.com/digital-marketing/

Sinan Soft (2019). *Advantages and Disadvantages of Digital Marketing.* Retrieved from https://sinansoft.com/blog/advantages-and-disadvantages-of-digital-marketing/

Hubspot (2019). *What is Guerilla Marketing? 7 Examples to Inspire Your Brand.* Retrieved from https://blog.hubspot.com/marketing/guerilla-marketing-examples

Think Premium (2017). *What Do the Pros and Cons of Guerilla Marketing Mean for Your Business.* Retrieved from https://thinkpremiumja.wordpress.com/2017/05/15/what-do-the-pros-and-cons-of-guerrilla-marketing-mean-for-your-business/

Tech Target (2019). *Relationship Marketing.* Retrieved from https://searchcustomerexperience.techtarget.com/definition/relationship-marketing

Chron (2019). *Advantages & Disadvantages of Customer Relationship Marketing.* Retrieved from https://smallbusiness.chron.com/advantages-disadvantages-customer-relationship-marketing-45503.html

Investopedia (2019). *Word-of-Mouth Marketing (WOM).* Retrieved from https://www.investopedia.com/terms/w/word-of-mouth-marketing.asp

Marketing-Schools.org (2019). *Word of Mouth Marketing.* Retrieved from https://www.marketing-schools.org/types-of-marketing/word-of-mouth-marketing.html

Chron (2019). *Pros & Cons of Word of Mouth Marketing.* Retrieved from https://smallbusiness.chron.com/pros-cons-word-mouth-marketing-52484.html

Chron (2019). *What is an Example of Transactional Marketing?* Retrieved from https://smallbusiness.chron.com/example-transactional-marketing-25886.html

eHow UK (2019). *What are the advantages & Disadvantages of Transactional Marketing?* Retrieved from https://www.ehow.co.uk/info_8087208_advantages-disadvantages-transactional-marketing.html

The Balance (2019). *What Every Nonprofit and Company Should Know About Cause Marketing.* Retrieved from https://www.thebalancesmb.com/what-every-nonprofit-should-know-about-cause-marketing-2502005

National Center for The Middle Market (2019). *The Pros and Cons of Cause Marketing.* Retrieved from https://www.middlemarketcenter.org/expert-perspectives/the-pros-and-cons-of-cause-marketing

Marketing-Schools.org (2019). *Undercover Marketing.* Retrieved from https://www.marketing-schools.org/types-of-marketing/undercover-marketing.html

Marketing Wit (2019). *An Explanation of Stealth Marketing with Suitable Examples.* Retrieved from https://marketingwit.com/explanation-of-stealth-marketing-with-examples

Business Know-How (2019). *Marketing Methods – Determine Which One is Best.* Retrieved from https://www.businessknowhow.com/marketing/method.htm

Entrepreneur (2019). *What is Business Networking, Anyway?* Retrieved from https://www.entrepreneur.com/article/196758

The Balance (2019). *What is Business Networking & What are the Benefits?* Retrieved from https://www.thebalancesmb.com/what-is-business-networking-and-what-are-the-benefits-2947183

Entrepreneurship Facts (2019). *Top 9 Benefits of Networking in Business.* Retrieved from https://entrepreneurshipfacts.com/top-9-benefits-of-networking-in-business/

Your Story (2019). *13 Ways Business Owners Can Increase Their Network.* Retrieved from https://yourstory.com/2012/07/13-ways-business-owners-can-increase-their-network

Virginia Counseling (2019). *The Importance of a Support System.* Retrieved from http://www.vacounseling.com/building-support-system/

Avail (2019). *What is A Healthy Support System?* Retrieved from https://www.availnyc.org/healthy-support-system/

Lifehack (2019). *10 Reasons Why You Should Avoid Negative People.* Retrieved from https://www.lifehack.org/352233/10-reasons-why-you-should-avoid-negative-people

Scientific American (2019). *The Importance of Being Social.* Retrieved from https://blogs.scientificamerican.com/streams-of-consciousness/the-importance-of-being-social/

The World Counts (2019). *The Benefits of Social Support for Happiness.* Retrieved from https://www.theworldcounts.com/life/potentials/social-connections-and-happiness

The Oaks (2019). *Five Benefits of Social Interactions for Seniors.* Retrieved from https://oaksatdenville.org/blog/benefits-social-interactions/

Huffpost (2019). *Why All Entrepreneurs Need a Support System.* Retrieved from https://www.huffpost.com/entry/why-all-entrepreneurs-nee_b_12468772

Inc. (2019). *Entrepreneurs Need a Support System.* Retrieved from https://www.inc.com/replacemeplease1455988044.html

Inc. (2019). *5 benefits of Community for Entrepreneurs.* Retrieved from https://www.inc.com/murray-newlands/5-benefits-of-community-for-entrepreneurs.html

Business.com (2019). *How to Learn From Your Failures: 4 Valuable Lessons.* Retrieved from https://www.business.com/articles/learning-from-failure/

Wesst (2019). *Starting a Business Requires Personal Dedication.* Retrieved from https://www.wesst.org/2014/01/starting-a-business-requires-personal-dedication/

Motivation Grid 2019. *The Reason Why Hard Work Is The Key to Success.* https://motivationgrid.com/hard-work-is-the-key-to-success/

ASHTON EUGENE THOMAS

www.ingramcontent.com/pod-product-compliance
Lightning Source LLC
LaVergne TN
LVHW011153080426
835508LV00007B/383